Joseph C. Sweeney

D1214762

SEAN O'CASEY
and his world

DAVID KRAUSE

SEAN O'CASEY

and his world

THAMES AND HUDSON
LONDON

To EILEEN O'CASEY,
in memory of her darlin' husband Sean,
whose great good soul goes marching on

© 1976 Thames and Hudson Ltd,
London

All rights reserved. No part of
this publication may be reproduced
or transmitted in any form or by
any means, electronic or
mechanical, including photocopy,
recording or any information
storage and retrieval system,
without permission in writing
from the publisher.

Printed in Great Britain
by Butler & Tanner Ltd
Frome and London.

THE YOUNG SEAN O'CASEY was a founder-member of the St Laurence O'Toole Pipers' Band, and on one occasion the band had arranged to play at a special function outside Dublin. Since the members were expected to pay their own train fare, this meant that the unemployed and penniless Sean could not make the journey. When several of his friends volunteered to buy a ticket for him, 'Sean the Proud', as he was known in those days early in the century, replied in a phrase that might have characterized his whole life: 'I wouldn't go to heaven on a free ticket.' If he made it to heaven in the end, he paid his own way. The quality of his life and art was his ticket.

Proud, Protestant and poor, O'Casey was born in Dublin on 30 March 1880 at 85 Upper Dorset Street on the rough north side of the Liffey, a short distance from the house on Lower Dorset Street where Richard Brinsley Sheridan had been born, just around the corner from 7 Eccles Street where James Joyce's wandering Leopold Bloom had lived, close to Dion Boucicault's birthplace in Lower Gardiner Street, and near Brendan Behan's territory in Russell Street. Perhaps there was a literary aura in the air he breathed. He was the last of thirteen children born to Michael and Susan Casey, eight of whom had already died in infancy, mostly of the croup, a type of diphtheria prevalent among the Dublin poor. Joining three brothers and a sister as the only children fortunate

The port of Dublin in the 1880s: looking down-river from the Custom House.

5

This was the Dublin in which
the young Sean grew up.

to grow to adulthood, the thirteenth child was christened John,
but in his twenties when he learned the Irish language and took
up the cause of Irish freedom and culture he gaelicized his name
to Sean O'Cathasaigh, later anglicizing the surname to O'Casey
when the Abbey Theatre performed his first accepted play in 1923.

As a young man O'Casey was an unskilled labourer and naturally
identified himself with the working class, a proletarian conviction he
maintained throughout his life, but his parents were lower middle
class bordering on the edges of poverty. His father Michael, originally from Limerick, was the son of a mixed marriage, a Catholic
father and Protestant mother. After his father, an indigent farmer,
died at an early age, Michael's mother raised him, her last-born
and favourite child, in her own Protestant faith, but the rest of the
children remained devout Catholics. Perhaps it was to be expected
that religious tensions in the family often led to violent quarrels,
and after his mother died the outnumbered and alienated Michael
escaped to Dublin, where in 1863 he met and married Susan Archer,
the daughter of a Protestant auctioneer in Wicklow. He earned his
modest living as a commercial clerk, and for many years worked
for the Irish Church Mission, a proselytizing Protestant organization that would only have employed people who were dedicated to
the unpopular cause of 'Souperism' – as it was mockingly called by
the starving Catholics who had been offered free soup and Protestant salvation during the tragic Potato Famine of 1845–47. During
his last years when he was suffering from a spinal injury and was

O'Connell bridge, Dublin.

Bull Alley, in the Dublin slums.

The tenement house in Upper Dorset Street, Dublin, of which Sean's father was the caretaker and where Sean himself was born.

unable to work, Michael became caretaker of the tenement house in Upper Dorset Street, which meant free rent for the struggling family; but he died in 1886 at the age of forty-nine, when his youngest son was six years old, and thereafter the declining family situation grew worse.

The fatherless little Johnny was a sickly child who in infancy had contracted trachoma, a chronic eye disease which impaired his sight and prevented him from living a normal childhood. His weak and suppurating eyes had to be treated every day with soakings and ointments and bandages, which meant many years of regular trips with his mother to the public dispensary of St Mark's Ophthalmic Hospital, a demeaning experience that he shared with the destitute Catholics who usually filled the crowded waiting-room, though his proud mother was determined to pay the sixpence a month fee that was waived for the poor. For the bewildered boy it meant a psychological as well as a physical wound, to be isolated in semi-darkness, surrounded by human misery, and treated as a chronic invalid. For his courageous mother, a militant Protestant trying to survive on contributions from the wages of her older children and forced to measure out each penny, it was an ironic humiliation that the family had more in common with their poor Catholic neighbours than with the prosperous and generally aloof Protestants in the city, to many of whom poverty was merely the result of moral lassitude and therefore properly reserved for the Catholics. Thus the religion into which O'Casey had been born was itself an alienating factor, when one considers what it meant to exist at the lower levels of society as a Protestant in the Dublin of the 1880s where eighty per cent of the population of 250,000 were Catholic and predominantly poor, while most of the Protestant minority were well off or members of the gentry and titled Anglo-Irish. By the Protestant standards of social and economic status, therefore, the Casey family was a failure.

Formal education was an irregular and impossible experience for the half-blind youngest member of the family. Although he was sent to a Protestant church school for several years, he was often absent, forced to stay at home to have his eyes nursed or go to the hospital, and his poor eyesight prevented him from learning to read and write. Owing to the diligence of his mother, however, a devout church-goer who daily read the Bible to him, he had managed to memorize so many passages from scripture that when he was seven years old he won a Sunday School prize 'For Proficiency in Holy Scripture and Church Formularies'. When he was ten, with the help and encouragement of his older brother Archie who was active in a local amateur theatre group, he was memorizing speeches from the plays of Shakespeare and Boucicault, and the two Casey brothers often performed scenes together at neighbourhood parties.

Susan Casey, Sean's mother. She is holding a grandchild, daughter of Sean's sister Isabella.

Drama was therefore the first excitement of his early youth, and five years later he had an unexpected opportunity to act in public on a stage for the first time at the old Mechanics Theatre in Abbey Street. This was the same theatre which, nine years later in 1904, was to be taken over by W. B. Yeats and Lady Gregory and, with the adjoining city morgue, rebuilt as the Abbey Theatre. It happened that the touring company of Charles D'Alton, the Irish comedian and actor-manager, was scheduled to give a performance of

(*Above*) Playbill for Boucicault's *The Shaughraun*, and (*above, right*) a sketch by Jack Butler Yeats of the old Mechanics' Theatre. Here, and in this play, Sean first acted on a public stage.

Boucicault's *The Shaughraun* at the Mechanics Theatre, and when one of the actors suddenly became ill a distress call went out for a last-minute replacement. D'Alton's son Louis (later to become a popular playwright at the Abbey), who was in the company and who several years earlier had acted in scenes from Boucicault's plays with the Casey brothers in the local amateur group, called in the fifteen-year-old Johnny Casey, who was unusually tall and ascetic-looking for his age, and happened to know all the lines, to take over the role of Father Dolan, the patriotic priest who defends a Fenian rebel and comforts the oppressed people. He played the part on the stage where twenty-eight years later his own first accepted play, *The Shadow of a Gunman*, was to be performed by the Abbey Theatre company.

Meanwhile he had been teaching himself to read and write since his early teens, with help from his sister Isabella, who was a teacher at St Mary's school. When he was fourteen he earned his first money, three shillings and sixpence for a sixty-hour week, working as a stock boy for a wholesale chandlers' firm. In his twenties he was working at odd jobs as a common labourer with pick and shovel, and he began to frequent the Dublin bookstalls, gradually building his own library by buying and sometimes stealing second-hand copies of his favourite authors, the works of Shakespeare, Dickens, Scott, Balzac, Milton, Byron, Keats, Shelley, Goldsmith, Sheridan, Ruskin.

His intellectual and religious curiosity had also been stimulated by the Rev. Dr Edward Morgan Griffin, the Rector of St Barnabas Church, who became the father-figure of his youth. For a time he attended church services regularly, and at Dr Griffin's suggestion he briefly tried his hand at teaching Sunday School classes at St Barnabas. Many years later one of the Rector's daughters recollected her impressions of the young O'Casey around 1904, particularly his fervent behaviour at the prayer-meetings that her father held on weekday evenings in the Church schoolhouse. At the conclusion of the service the Rector would always ask for a volunteer to lead the final prayer. 'It was then,' she recalled, 'after an awkward pause while father waited for the volunteer, that my sister and I – we were girls of eight and ten – would nudge each other and whisper, "It'll be John again" – he was John to us, not Sean – "he'll jump up again, and oh, he'll go on and on as he always does." He sat behind us and we were afraid to turn around and look, but soon we heard his voice ringing out loud and clear, in that drawling, lilting way he had of speaking. He didn't read from the prayer-book as the others did, he just made up his prayer as he went along, using some biblical passages but mostly his own words about the glory of God. As I said, at the time my sister and I joked about how he would go on and on with it, but we were silly little girls then, and when I think of it all now it comes back to me as something very moving and beautiful. He would have made a great preacher.'

Perhaps he did become something of a great preacher, though he eventually lost his fervour for Christianity and went on to find the glory of God and man in the ideals of Irish freedom and culture, in the stirring sound of the Irish pipers, in the revival of the Irish language, in the amateur theatre movement, in the socialist crusade of Jim Larkin and the rise of the Irish labour movement, and subsequently in the tragicomic world of his plays and his monumental autobiography. He learned the Irish language and joined the Gaelic League; he learned to play the Irish war pipes and helped organize the St Laurence O'Toole Pipers' Band; he wrote songs and sketches which he sang and read at meetings of the O'Toole Club, and acted in plays performed by the Club's Dramatic Society; he joined the secret Irish Republican Brotherhood; he joined Larkin's new union for unskilled labourers, the Irish Transport and General Workers' Union.

Rev. Dr Griffin, Rector of St Barnabas Church and father-figure of Sean's youth.

The St Laurence O'Toole Pipers' Band in 1913. The bare-headed marcher on the left is Sean O'Casey.

Ireland which is, And I who am Ireland Have not Forgotten You

Christmas 1921.

From:
Address.

When Jim Larkin, the Irish labour leader, was jailed in America, Sean designed this Christmas card, to be sent to the prisoner as a mark of solidarity by friends and sympathizers.

Most of all, however, words became the weapons of his idealism and discontent in downtrodden Dublin. During the first two decades of the century he wrote many articles and letters in defence of freedom and socialism, mainly for Larkin's newspaper, the *Irish Worker*; and he soon became known as the champion secretary, wielding his pen as secretary of the St Laurence O'Toole Athletic and Dramatic Club, secretary of the St Laurence O'Toole Pipers' Band, secretary of the Red Hand Hurling Club, secretary of the Drumcondra Branch of the Gaelic League, secretary of the Women and Children's Relief Fund during the 1913 general strike and lock-out, secretary of the Wolfe Tone Memorial Committee, secretary of the Irish Citizen Army, secretary of the Release Jim Larkin Committee.

In later years, when he was asked why he lost his faith in the Church, he replied without hesitation, 'I never lost my faith, I found it. I found it when Jim Larkin came to Dublin and organized the unskilled workers. I found it in Jim's great socialist motto: "An injury to one is the concern of all". He was the saviour of Dublin. He put his faith in the people and their need to live a better and fuller life. And that's where I put my faith.'

The dynamic Larkin was probably the most important influence on the young O'Casey and the shaping of his proletarian view of life; Larkin the liberator, the 'Prometheus Hibernica' of O'Casey's autobiography, the fiery street orator and heroic union leader who came to Dublin to eliminate some of the worst slums in Europe and protect the people from the money-changers with his 'divine mission of discontent'. When Larkin went to London in 1913 to address a huge labour rally in the Albert Hall to gain support for the Dublin strikers, the novelist David Garnett was present and wrote a vivid description of the mighty figure in action: 'There, striding about the platform one beheld the whole of the sweated, starved, exploited working class suddenly incarnate in the shape of a gigantic Tarzan of all the slum jungles of the West.'

For Irish nationalists the Easter Rising of 1916 was the crucial event in Irish history; but for the Irish working class, and for O'Casey, Larkin's general strike of 1913 had launched the first blow for the liberation of the Irish people. As he did throughout his life, O'Casey put his socialism before his nationalism, and he turned out for the strike but not for the Rising. He chose to be a rebel worker rather than a rebel patriot. Though he was active in the strike and served directly with Larkin in the union headquarters at Liberty Hall, and became secretary of Labour's Irish Citizen Army, the militant wing of the union organized to protect the people from

Sean at thirty, moustached and in his Sunday best.

Jim Larkin, fiery street orator, trade union leader, and Sean's hero.

The Easter Rising, 1916: barricade in Brunswick Street.

Viewing the destruction, after the Rising.

The gutted G.P.O., Dublin – headquarters of the rebels.

A socialist first and a nationalist afterwards, Sean drew these ironical sketches of the Rising to illustrate one of his letters.

police brutality, he ultimately resigned from the Army in protest against those middle-class nationalists who had been unsympathetic to the strike and were now, he believed, undermining the cause of economic freedom. Although he was enthusiastic about the Gaelic principles of Padraic Pearse, who was to become one of the martyrs of the Rising, O'Casey was furious when he learned that Pearse had been a strike-breaker in 1913, regularly using the 'black' trams. O'Casey believed that the national movement for independence had to be rooted in the socialist principles of Larkin and the working class.

Some years later Augustus John, the Welsh artist who had painted a portrait of O'Casey, was distressed by the playwright's proud working-class loyalties and wrote to him in 1929: 'I don't see why you need to attach yourself to any *class*. A poet, an artist is really no class at all.' Such a detached view of the artist might have been all right for some art-for-art's-sake aesthetes or littérateurs of independent means, but O'Casey could not have been an artist at all if he had not as a man of conscience attached himself, by experience and by conviction, to the working class. For him there was no such thing as a classless artist, or a classless man. For him the artist even more than the ordinary man had a responsibility to his fellow men which was inseparable from his responsibility to his art.

This double responsibility is apparent everywhere in his life, and in everything he wrote, in his early articles, his pamphlets and booklets of songs, his plays and books of essays, his letters and his autobiography. In *Red Roses For Me*, for example, when his autobiographical hero, Ayamonn Breydon, a creative young labourer who is a leader in a city-wide strike, and who attends a church called St Burnupus where he is a close friend of the Rector, joins the common people of Dublin in a mythic dance of transformation on the banks of the Liffey and exhorts them to fulfil their miraculous dream, he expresses that double vision of great art and the good life:

Friend, we would that you should live a greater life; we will that all of us shall live a greater life. Our strike is yours. A step ahead for us today; another one for you tomorrow. We who have known, and know, the emptiness of life shall know its fullness. All men and women quick with life are fain to venture forward. The apple grows for you to eat. The violet grows for you to wear. Young maiden, another world is in your womb ... Our city's in th' grip o' God.

This biblical diction and rhythm coloured everything he wrote, though he usually complemented it with a heady mixture of tragicomic irony and hilarious knockabout. But the life of the Dublin slums that he dramatized was more often in the grip of war than the grip of God, the decade of the Irish war of economic and political independence and civil strife, from 1913 to 1923, much of which provides the 'terrible beauty' of his Dublin trilogy, *The Shadow of a Gunman* (1923), *Juno and the Paycock* (1924), *The Plough and the Stars* (1926). With these three plays he established himself as one of the major figures in modern drama.

His struggle toward artistic recognition was an ordeal that would have defeated a man of less courage and fierce determination, for he had to overcome the disappointment of four rejected manuscripts before the Abbey Theatre finally accepted the *Gunman*. And it should also be remembered that the Abbey's new playwright was forty-three years old when he launched his career; that he was still working as a labourer during the three-day run of the play, which

In this ill-lit tenement at 422
North Circular Road, Dublin,
Sean lived from 1921 to 1925,
and here he wrote his first three
plays.

Sean in 1924, after the decision to give up his labouring job and earn his living from writing alone.

Armed with pen and ink, Sean goes forth to battle.

earned him the sum of four pounds in royalties, even though it played to packed houses and the 'House Full' sign had to be hung out on the final night for the first time in the twenty-year history of the Abbey. A year later *Juno and the Paycock* was even more successful and had to be extended for a second week, the first time an Abbey play had run longer than one week. O'Casey had arrived in time to save the languishing Abbey Theatre from artistic and financial bankruptcy, but he was still working as a cement mixer on a road repair job until he received the princely fortune of twenty-five pounds after the two-week run. So at the age of forty-four he finally decided to give up his job and for the remaining forty years of his life earned his precarious living by his pen alone.

In an early letter to his Dublin friend Gabriel Fallon, he drew a sketch of himself armed with pen and ink as he went forth into the battle of life. This fighting posture turned out to be a prophetic image, since he was destined to be a controversial figure who raised the most sensitive issues of Irish history and humanity and consequently had to defend himself and his work from many of his

Rehearsal in the old Abbey Theatre.

This self-portrait shows the alarm clock and the crowing cock reminding Sean of Time's hurrying footsteps. The beard was grown during a short stay in hospital.

THE SHADOW
OF A
GUNMAN

Cartoons by Grace Plunkett in the Abbey Theatre programme of *The Shadow of a Gunman*.

irate countrymen throughout his life. His first two accepted plays were as provocative as they were popular, for his uninhibited tenement characters consistently profaned the fanatical aspects of the nationalist idealism when they mockingly questioned the revolutionary rhetoric of the patriots which inevitably led to the slaughter of innocent people. Seumas Shields, the comic-ironic pedlar in *The Shadow of a Gunman*, objects to the indiscriminate bloodshed in 1920 during the guerrilla warfare between the insurgent Irish Republican Army and the British troops, and speaking as a Catholic his words have a terrible relevance to the strife-torn Ireland of the 1970s:

I wish to God it was over. The country is gone mad. Instead of counting their beads now they're countin' bullets; their Hail Marys and paternosters are burstin' bombs – burstin' bombs, an' the rattle of machine-guns; petrol is their holy water; their Mass is a burnin' buildin'; their De Profundis is 'The Soldier's Song', an' their creed is, 'I believe in the gun almighty, maker of heaven an' earth' – an' it's all for 'the glory o' God an' the honour o' Ireland'.

When his friend, the poet Davoren, says to him, 'I remember the time when you yourself believed in nothing but the gun,' Shields replies pointedly, 'Ay, when there wasn't a gun in the country; I've a different opinion now when there's nothing but guns in the country.' And then Shields goes on to disassociate himself from the brutality of the gunmen as well as the tyranny of the British subjugation of Ireland:

It's the civilians who suffer; when there's an ambush they don't know where to run. Shot in the back to save the British Empire, an' shot in the breast to save the soul of Ireland. I'm a Nationalist meself, right enough – a Nationalist right enough, but all the same – I'm a Nationalist right enough; I believe in the freedom of Ireland, an' that England has no right to be here, but I draw the line when I hear the gunmen blowin' about dyin' for the people, when it's the people that are dyin' for the gunmen! With all due respect to the gunmen, I don't want them to die for me.

No amount of nationalistic rhetoric could make O'Casey overlook the fact that the dead non-combatants in the city far outnumbered

(*Left*) Arthur Sinclair as Seumas Shields in *The Shadow of a Gunman* – the voice of the suffering civilian in a strife-torn Ireland – at the Court Theatre, London, in June 1927. (*Right*) Eileen Carey as Minnie, frantically hiding the bombs from the Black and Tans. Three months later, she and Sean were married.

the dead gunmen. And since he was a working-class rebel with dreams of a socialist republic for Ireland, he had reason to be sceptical about a middle-class insurrection with its patriotic principles and fanatical gunmen who glorified the terror of a holy war that was devouring its children. In *Juno and the Paycock*, the action of which is set in 1922 during the Civil War between the supporters of the new Irish Free State government and the diehard Republican Army which rejected the compromise treaty of partition, the argument over sacrificial principles arises often in the destitute Boyle family. 'Captain' Jack Boyle, the strutting 'paycock', and his parasite 'buttie' Joxer Daly, the mock-heroic jesters who manage to dominate much of the action with their mendacious antics, are only interested in the comic principle of self-preservation at any price.

'The whole counthry's in a state o' chassis': Arthur Sinclair as 'Captain' Jack Boyle in *Juno and the Paycock*.

The Royalty Theatre, London, presented the *Paycock* in 1925, with the original Abbey company.

ROYALTY ♔ THEATRE

Licensed by the Lord Chamberlain to DENNIS EADIE.

Every Evening at 8.30

DENNIS EADIE and J. B. FAGAN

PRESENT

(By arrangement with the Directors of the Abbey Theatre, Dublin)

Juno and the Paycock

BY

SEAN O'CASEY

"Captain" Jack Boyle - - -	ARTHUR SINCLAIR
Juno Boyle, *his wife* - - -	SARA ALLGOOD
Johnny Boyle ⎱ *their children* ⎰ -	HARRY HUTCHINSON
Mary Boyle ⎰ ⎱ -	KATHLEEN O'REGAN
"Joxer" Daly - - -	SYDNEY MORGAN
Mrs. Maisie Madigan - - -	MAIRE O'NEILL
"Needle" Nugent, *a tailor* - -	J. A. O'ROURKE
Mrs. Tancred - - -	KITTY KIRWAN
Jerry Devine - - -	DAVID MORRIS
Charlie Bentham, *a school teacher* -	ERIC PAGE
An Irregular Mobilizer - -	BARNEY MULLIGAN
An Irregular - - -	E. J. KENNEDY
A Coal Block Vendor - -	EDMUND O'GRADY
A Sewing Machine Man - -	CHRISTOPHER STEELE
Furniture Removal Man - -	EDMUND O'GRADY
Two Neighbours - - -	⎰ MOLLIE MACKAY ⎱ JOYCE CHANCELLOR

The Play produced by J. B. FAGAN

'Are you goin' to do in a comrade?—look at me arm, I lost it for Ireland.' Johnny Boyle is dragged out by the Irregulars to his death.

These two braggart clowns, who have their ancestry in Roman and Elizabethan comedy, are as irresistible as they are irresponsible, and they reflect O'Casey's ironic attitude toward heroism.

In the parallel tragic action of the play, when Johnny Boyle, who had his hip crippled in the Easter Rising and lost an arm fighting with the IRA in the Civil War, asserts that he would do it all again and give his life for Ireland because 'a principle's a principle', his mother Juno promptly takes her own stand on such heroics:

Ah, you lost your best principle, me boy, when you lost your arm; them's the only sort o' principles that's any good to a workin' man.

Sara Allgood as Juno Boyle.

Juno Boyle is O'Casey's universal mother, and like most of the real-istic and compassionate women who appear in his works she places her faith in the basic human situation rather than in the sentimental abstractions that lead inevitably to death and martyrdom. Towards the end of the play when her terrorized son is shot for betraying Hughie Tancred, an IRA comrade, Juno follows the earlier prayer of Mrs Tancred and keens a classic lament for her poor dead son:

What was the pain I suffered, Johnny, bringin' you into the world to carry you to your cradle, to the pains I'll suffer carryin' you out o' the world to bring you to your grave! Mother o' God, Mother o' God, have pity on us all! Blessed Virgin, where were you when me darlin' son was riddled with bullets, when me darlin' son was riddled with bullets? Sacred Heart o' Jesus, take away our hearts o' stone, and give us hearts o' flesh! Take away this murdherin' hate, an' give us Thine own eternal love!

But the prayer was not to be answered, and in light of O'Casey's consistent refusal to idealize the violence it was no surprise that his next play, *The Plough and the Stars*, provoked a riot in the Abbey Theatre when groups of diehard nationalists interrupted the performance with a wild demonstration against his ironic treatment of the Easter Rising. According to the outraged rioters, O'Casey had insulted the nation by deflating the patriots and concentrating on his own working-class Dublin, especially the tragicomic men, women and sickly children of the now bullet-riddled tenements. He was also accused of desecrating the sacred Republican flag by allowing it to be brought into a pub, and of defiling the honour of Irish womanhood by portraying an Irish girl as a prostitute. Furthermore, in the second act the actual words of the martyred Padraic Pearse had been exposed to mock-heroic irony. While the messianic Pearse-figure is outside the pub calling the people to join him in a ritualistic blood-sacrifice, preaching his sermon on 'the sanctity of bloodshed' and 'the exhilaration of war', the earthy characters of the slums are inside the pub drinking and brawling in a series of farcical battles about respectability. Throughout the play the frailty and humanity of these magnificently rude mechanicals, led by Fluther Good, Ginnie Gogan, Bessie Burgess, Peter Flynn and The Covey, mock the holiness of the war. We are in no doubt about O'Casey's irony when Commandant Jack Clitheroe and two of his comrades appear in full-dress uniform, after they have been mesmerized by the words of Pearse, and they solemnly announce their patriotic principles:

CLITHEROE   You have a mother, Langon.
LIEUT. LANGON   Ireland is greater than a mother.
CAPT. BRENNAN   You have a wife, Clitheroe.
CLITHEROE   Ireland is greater than a wife.

But Clitheroe's wife Nora later replies for the mothers and wives of Ireland when she returns after an unsuccessful attempt to find her husband in the barricaded streets:

An' there's no woman gives a son or a husband to be killed – if they say it, they're lyin', lyin', against God, Nature, an' against themselves.

Apparently the rioters in the Abbey Theatre disagreed with the principles of Nora Clitheroe. After an initial uproar of booing and catcalling and the singing of patriotic songs during the second act which reduced the actors to mere dumb-show, the play was stopped completely in the third act when curses, vegetables, shoes and chairs were hurled at the stage and stench bombs were set off in the theatre. The curtain was lowered, the police were called in to restore order, and W. B. Yeats, director of the Abbey, Irish Senator and Nobel

ABBEY THEATRE
— DUBLIN. —

Proprietors — THE NATIONAL THEATRE SOCIETY, Ltd
Directors — W. B. YEATS, LADY GREGORY,
GEORGE O'BRIEN, LENNOX ROBINSON
Manager — MICHAEL J. DOLAN

Producer — LENNOX ROBINSON
Assistant Producer — ARTHUR SHIELDS
Stage Manager — F. J. McCORMICK

All seats in Theatre with exception of Back Pit may be Booked
Seats Reserved by Telephone and not paid for, will not be kept
later than 7.45 p.m.   Telephone 3268

Monday, Feb. 8th, 1926, and following nights at **8**
Matinee, Saturday, at 2.30

FIRST PRODUCTION OF
THE PLOUGH AND THE STARS
A Tragedy in Four Acts, by SEAN O'CASEY

Characters

COMMANDANT JACK CLITHEROE	
(of the Irish Citizen Army)	F. J. McCormick
NORA CLITHEROE (his wife)	Shelah Richards
PETER FLYNN (Nora's uncle)	Eric Gorman
THE YOUNG COVEY (Clitheroe's cousin)	Michael J. Dolan
FLUTHER GOOD	Barry Fitzgerald
BESSIE BURGESS	Maureen Delany
MRS. GOGAN (a charwoman)	May Craig
MOLLSER (her consumptive daughter)	Kitty Curling
CAPTAIN BRENNAN (of the I.C.A.)	Gabriel J. Fallon
LIEUT. LANGON (of the Irish Volunteers)	Arthur Shields
ROSIE REDMOND	Ria Mooney
A BARMAN	P. J. Carolan
A WOMAN	Eileen Crowe
THE VOICE	J. Stephenson
CORPORAL STODDARD (of the Wiltshires)	P. J. Carolan
SERGEANT TINLEY (of the Wiltshires)	J. Stephenson

NOTICE—Owing to numerous Complaints, the Management must insist that ladies Sitting in the Stalls shall remove their hats

ACT I. Scene - The living room of the Clitheroe's three-room flat in a tenement house in Dublin

ACT II. Scene - A corner public-house in the street where a meeting is being held

ACT III. Scene - The outside of the tenement house in which Clitheroes live

ACT IV. Scene - Bessie Burgess's room in the same tenement

A few hours elapse between Acts I. and II. Some months between Acts II. and III. and a few days between Acts III. and IV

Period of Play - Acts I. and II. November 1915; Acts III. and IV. Easter Week 1916

The Orchestra, under the Direction of Dr. J. F. LARCHET, will perform the following selections :

Overture	"Mireila"	Gounod (1818-1893)
Fantasy	"La Bohème"	Puccini (1858-1924)
Slow Movement	"The New World" Symphony	Dvořák (1841-1904)
Irish Reel	"Molly on the Shore"	Grainger (b. 1882)

ANNOUNCEMENT
Tuesday, February 16th, 1926, and following nights at 8
Matinee Saturday, at 2.30

DOCTOR KNOCK
By JULES ROMAIN

TEA ROOMS IN VESTIBULE
CHOCOLATES, ETC.

REFRESHMENTS WILL BE SERVED IN
THEATRE IF DESIRED

Rioting, boos and catcalls greeted *The Plough and the Stars* at the Abbey. The author's irony was too much for the diehard nationalists.

Sean O'Casey with Ria Mooney, who played the prostitute Rosie Redmond. Sean wrote on this photograph, 'Be clever, my gal, & let who will be good.'

W. B. Yeats: portrait by his father.

Yeats addressing the audience of angry puritans at the Abbey Theatre in 1907, when they howled down Synge's *Playboy of the Western World*.

Prize poet, strode majestically to the stage to celebrate O'Casey's play by defying the mob of irate patriots, just as he had celebrated Synge's *Playboy of the Western World* in 1907 by defying a mob of irate puritans:

You have disgraced yourselves again. Is this to be an ever-recurring celebration of the arrival of Irish genius? Synge first and then O'Casey. The news of the happenings of the past few minutes will go from country to country. Dublin has once more rocked the cradle of genius. From such a scene in this theatre went forth the fame of Synge. Equally the fame of O'Casey is born here tonight. This is his apotheosis.

At the time O'Casey did not know what the word 'apotheosis' meant, but he knew that he was beginning to feel like an exile in his native land. Even before the riot, during rehearsals, he had been confronted by a backstage rebellion of the actors who refused to say some of his 'vulgar' dialogue and generally objected to playing

John Millington Synge: portrait
by Jack Butler Yeats.

his rough tenement characters. Two members of the Abbey board
of directors did not want to produce the play at all and only relented
when some changes were made in the script: for the sake of Irish
prudery the love scene between the Clitheroes in Act One was
'toned down'; the randy song at the end of Act Two was eliminated,
and has in fact to this day never been sung in revivals of the play
at the Abbey; so-called 'blasphemous' and 'vituperative' expres-
sions were modified. After the riot O'Casey was forced to defend
his play in a letter-writing controversy and public debate in which
he was reviled and humiliated. Many reactions to the play were
favourable, but many reviews and letters to the press hurled accusa-
tions of 'Sewage School drama', 'Dirt for dirt's sake', 'cheap music-
hall concoction', and O'Casey himself was called 'a guttersnipe from
the slums'. He replied to some of these charges, in one letter objecting that the prudes and patriots 'are determined to make of Ireland
the terrible place of a land fit only for heroes to live in'. And later

Sean in London, in 1926. Behind him is a poster of the West End production of *Juno*.

in his autobiography he recorded this impression of his disenchantment with the raging Kathleen ni Houlihan:

For the first time in his life, Sean felt a surge of hatred for Kathleen ni Houlihan sweeping over him. He saw now that the one who had the walk of a queen could be a bitch at times. She galled the hearts of her children who dared to be above the ordinary, and she often slew her best ones. She had hounded Parnell to death; she had yelled and torn at Yeats, at Synge, and now she was doing the same to him. What an old snarly gob she could be at times; an ignorant one too.

Six weeks after the riot, in March 1926, he went to London to receive the Hawthornden Prize for *Juno*, and to oversee the West End production of the play. He had no immediate intention of forsaking Ireland at the time, since he had paid the rent for his tenement room in Dublin up to May and continued to write faithfully to his friends at home. Nevertheless, he was enjoying his new freedom in London, away from the bitterness of Dublin; he was developing new friendships with men like Bernard Shaw and Augustus John; and in May he had fallen in love with Eileen Carey, the

Sean with Augustus John, who painted his portrait.

Lennox Robinson, director of the Abbey Theatre with Yeats and Lady Gregory.

Yeats and Lady Gregory in the grounds of her house, Coole Park.

(*Opposite*) Sean and Eileen O'Casey on their wedding day, 23 September 1927, outside the church of All Souls and the Redeemer, Chelsea.

beautiful young Irish-born actress who was playing the role of Nora Clitheroe in the London production of *Plough*. In 1927 he married Miss Carey, and he was finishing a new play, *The Silver Tassie*, which was to touch off another bitter controversy when it was rejected by Yeats and the Abbey Theatre. This crucial event was to have an irrevocably damaging effect upon the career of O'Casey and the future of the Abbey; he was deprived of an intimate relationship with a working theatre for the rest of his life and thereafter had to write his plays for publication prior to uncertain production; and meanwhile the Abbey lost the opportunity to produce the new plays of Ireland's greatest living dramatist.

While he had been distressed by the prudery of the Abbey actors, his quarrel over the *Plough* riot in 1926 had really been with rabid Irish nationalism not with Yeats, Lady Gregory and Lennox Robinson, the three friendly directors who had defended him and his play. Furthermore, his first three plays were now the cornerstone of the theatre's repertoire and it needed him as much as he needed it, since his works usually played to full houses and he depended on the royalties from regular revivals. It was understandable, therefore, that Lady Gregory and Robinson, especially, expressed their eager anticipation as they waited for the script of the new play. O'Casey himself was so confident the play would be accepted that he sent a recommended cast of actors to Robinson, suggesting F. J. McCormick for the leading role of Harry Heegan and Barry Fitzgerald for the comic role of Sylvester Heegan. In his letters to Lady Gregory he was full of excitement over the performance of his new play in Ireland, for even though he was living in London he still considered himself an Irish playwright with deep commitments to his country and the Abbey. 'I'll send on a copy to The Abbey,' he wrote to Lady Gregory in February 1928, '& will send a copy to no-one else till I get word that the play has been received, so that I may be able to say that The Abbey Theatre was the first to get my new effort.'

Lady Gregory was his most loyal and intimate friend at the Abbey, for she had been first to recognize and champion his genius, always including comments of encouragement when his early manuscripts were returned. If she was the fairy godmother of the Abbey, she was also O'Casey's fairy godmother. They liked each other instinctively from the start, this unlikely couple, the aristocratic lady and the plebeian playwright, and she became his dear companion and confidante from 1923 until she died in 1932. He wrote a moving tribute to her in his autobiography, in the chapter called 'Blessed Bridget O'Coole', and in one passage where he recalled his first meeting with her he drew this vivid portrait:

There she was, a sturdy, stout little figure soberly clad in solemn black, made gay with a touch of something white under a long, soft, black silk veil that covered her grey hair and flowed gracefully behind half-way down her back. A simple brooch shyly glistened under her throat, like a bejewelled lady making her first retreat, feeling a little ashamed of it. Her face was a rugged one, hardy as that of a peasant, curiously lit with an odd dignity, and softened with a careless touch of humour in the bright eyes and the curving wrinkles crowding around the corners of the firm little mouth. She looked like an old, elegant nun of a new order, a blend of the Lord Jesus Christ and of Puck, an order that Ireland had never known before, and wasn't likely to know again for a long time to come.

He wrote over forty letters to her in which he opened his heart about his ideas on literature, religion and politics, and his high hopes for the future of the Abbey and Irish culture. Twice he was her guest for ten days at her home at Coole Park in Galway, and he carved his initials alongside those of many notable figures on the familiar copper beech tree in her garden. When she invited him for his first visit in 1924, he wrote to thank her, and to comment on her book, *Our Irish Theatre*, about the early struggles of the Abbey Theatre:

I have just re-read your *Irish Theatre*, & have harboured a feeling of regret that I wasn't with the Abbey in the great fight that did so much for Ireland's Soul and Ireland's body.

I have been thinking about Synge, Hugh Lane, Robert Gregory – standing on the galley deck in *The Shadowy Waters*, 'blue & dim, with sails & dresses of green and ornaments of copper' – and Ledwidge, the young, pale poet; all now of the dead; and you, Yeats, Stephens & Shaw, still, happily, of the living. Aristocrats, middle-class and worker: 'Three in One & one in three.' When one remembers those that have died; & these that still live, one, when

Four leading lights of the Abbey Theatre: this sketch by Sir William Orpen shows Sir Hugh Lane, Synge, Yeats and Lady Gregory.

LADY GREGORY

SIGHING FOR NEW WORLDS TO KILTARTANISE.

Lady Gregory, Sean's most loyal friend at the Abbey, 'a sturdy, stout little figure soberly clad in solemn black'. Having translated Molière's comedies into the Kiltartan speech of Galway, she is affectionately caricatured as looking for more victims, having 'done' the Koran and Gregorian chants.

thinking of Ireland, can still murmur: blessed is the womb that bore them, & the paps that they have sucked.

He joined the Irish trinity of writers with her and they shared many triumphs at the revitalized Abbey. Four years later, when he sent the ill-fated manuscript of *The Silver Tassie* to Lady Gregory early in 1928, he added a reassuring P.S., remembering the riot over the *Plough*, 'There's no mention of politics throughout the play.' But it was the literary politics of Yeats not the nationalistic politics of the IRA which provoked the new controversy. And at this time a series of heart-breaking ironies began to develop in O'Casey's relationship with Lady Gregory. On the 28th of March, three weeks before the Abbey directors, Yeats, Lady Gregory and Robinson,

Coole Park.

The trunk of the copper beech tree in the garden at Coole Park bore many notable initials, including S O'C and WBY.

(*Opposite*) Lady Gregory: portrait by John Butler Yeats, the elder, painted in 1903 when she was fifty.

formally rejected the play, O'Casey wrote a beautifully poignant letter to Lady Gregory, a letter overflowing with great confidence and personal tribute to her. She had previously written to him in a state of deep depression – in all likelihood she already knew that the Abbey had decided against his play and perhaps she had allowed this knowledge to darken her thoughts, without revealing her painful secret. One can imagine, therefore, how the poor woman felt when she read this letter:

My dear Lady Gregory: – Now, now, now; you shouldn't be sad. It is hardly just to the mind & the vitality that have done so much for Coole & Galway; for Ireland and for womanhood. Shaw once said that you were the most distinguished of living Irishwomen. And now I have a thought of our present-day country women, seeking some, seeking even one, that had in her something of Grania, or Emer, or of Maeve, but God, perhaps, has hidden them from mine eyes. And you are with us still, still in front of our women, though no chair has been placed for you in the Senate or the Dail. And, apart from your own personal work altogether, you have done for Art & Literature, not only as much as Ireland would permit, but a great deal more than Ireland would permit you to do. And from what I know of you, – and I know you fairly well now – I don't believe you'll ever really grow old, for there always was, & always will be, a lot of the child in your soul. Like my mother, who aged & aged, but kept her keen, bright eyes, her intelligent mind & her humourful laugh for ever. And one thing is certain – that so long as God or Nature leaves us one atom of strength, we must continue to use that atom of strength to fight on for that which is above & before all governments & parties – Art & Literature which are the mantle & mirror of the Holy Ghost, and the sword of the Spirit.

My dear Lady Gregory you can always walk on with your head up. And remember you had to fight against your birth into position & comfort as others had to fight against their birth into hardship & poverty, & it is as difficult to come out of one as it is to come out of the other so that power may be gained to bring fountains and waters out of the hard rocks. My best Wishes to all at Coole.

Yours Affectionately, Sean.

Perhaps those people who speculate about the nature of O'Casey's politics do well to remember that although he was determined all his life to fight for improved living conditions for the working class, he was primarily an artist determined 'to fight on for that which is above & before all governments & parties – Art & Literature which are the mantle & mirror of the Holy Ghost, and the sword of the Spirit'. Even though he may have lost this initial fight over *The Silver Tassie*, he never relented in his effort 'to bring fountains and waters out of the hard rocks'. And the ironies continue, for on the same day that Yeats wrote the formal letter of rejection, 20 April 1928, O'Casey had once more written to Lady Gregory full of excitement about his new play and his return to

32, CLAREVILLE STREET, KENSINGTON, S.W.7.

TELEPHONE KENSINGTON 0600

Yeats: We decree that thou art a heretic.

Robbie: Cast out from the unity of the Abbey.

Yeats: Sundered from her body.

Robbie: Segregated and abandoned for evermore

Lady Gregory: Amen.

Ireland. But the three Fates at the Abbey were against it. Yeats and Robinson said no, the play was unworthy of production, and the reluctant Lady Gregory went along with them, though she had misgivings and recorded in her journal that it was a tragic mistake. Two years earlier a defiant Yeats had assailed the rioting Irish mob for its disgraceful behaviour and failure to appreciate the genius of O'Casey; but now it was an ailing Yeats, just back from a recuperation in Rapallo, who disgraced himself and his theatre.

At the eleventh hour Yeats made an ill-advised attempt, through the shaken Lady Gregory, to tell O'Casey he could make a public announcement that he himself had decided to withdraw his play for revisions, thus being spared the humiliation of an outright rejection. But this inept gesture of appeasement only added fuel to the fire. 'There is going to be no damned secrecy with me surrounding the Abbey's rejection of the play,' O'Casey wrote to Robinson, moving the centre of the argument away from Lady Gregory. 'Does [Yeats] think that I would practise in my life the prevarication and wretchedness that I laugh at in my plays?' Then poor Lady Gregory, no doubt acting out of an unrelieved sense of guilt, sent copies of all the Abbey correspondence related to the rejection on to

When *The Silver Tassie* was turned down by the Abbey, Yeats mistakenly tried to give O'Casey a face-saving formula. Charles Kelly's cartoon in the *Irish Statesman*, to which Sean had sent a full account of the affair, translates this as 'I suggest you tell the Press that my foot slipped.'

Sean's own version of the episode (*above, right*) shows the three directors pronouncing sentence of excommunication. YEATS: We decree that thou art a heretic. ROBBIE: Cast out from the unity of the Abbey. YEATS: Sundered from her body. ROBBIE: Segregated and abandoned for evermore. LADY GREGORY: Amen.

O'Casey, in a well-meaning but vain hope that the record of their deliberations might soften the blow. Whereupon the unrepentant O'Casey, prompted by his wounded pride and an urgent need for vindication, immediately sent all the letters, together with his own blistering reply to Yeats, to the London *Observer* and the *Irish Statesman* and the whole controversy was out in the open.

The duel between Yeats and O'Casey became a headline feature in all the papers. Yeats believed that O'Casey had unwisely forsaken the themes and techniques of his previous plays, O'Casey insisted that he refused to go on repeating the formula of past successes. O'Casey felt he had created something new, a universal anti-war play based on the horrors of World War I, written in an experimental fusion of surrealistic and naturalistic techniques that opened up rich possibilities for the theatre of the future. He was following in the Expressionistic path of Strindberg, O'Neill, Toller, and what was to become one of the main currents of non-realistic modern drama. He knew only too well that Yeats himself was freely experimenting with dance plays in verse after the ritualistic tradition of the Japanese Noh theatre; and that Lady Gregory was experimenting with folk history plays and wonder plays, as well as translating the comedies of Molière into the Kiltartan idiom of the Galway peasants. He had reason to remember from his reading of *Our Irish Theatre* that Lady Gregory had printed the original statement of principles in which she and Yeats had described their new Irish theatre as one that welcomed 'that freedom to experiment which is not found in the theatre of England, and without which no new movement in art or literature can succeed'. And it must have been especially ironic for him to recall that Lady Gregory had also written in her book, when justifying her search for new dramatic forms, 'The desire to experiment is like a fire in the blood.'

There was plenty of fire in O'Casey's blood now, but the main target of his indignation was Yeats, the magisterial poet who in his letter of rejection had read a lecture to O'Casey on the immutable Yeatsian rules of drama:

But you are not interested in the Great War; you never stood on its battle-fields or walked its hospitals, and so write out of your opinions.

The mere greatness of the war has thwarted you; it has refused to become mere background, and obtrudes itself upon the stage as so much dead wood that will not burn with the dramatic fire. Dramatic action is a fire that must burn up everything but itself; there should be no room in a play for anything that does not belong to it; the whole history of the world must be reduced to wallpaper in front of which the characters must pose and speak. Among the things that dramatic action must burn up are the author's opinions.

In his defence O'Casey had characteristically replied with a burning fire of his own, perhaps in the spirit of Blake's hot impulse that

This caricature of Yeats by
Edmund Dulac was drawn in
1915; the magisterial poet was
perhaps stronger then in
defending freedom to experiment
than when he turned thumbs
down to *The Silver Tassie*.

'The tygers of wrath are wiser than the horses of instruction', and
he shot back the following blast:

Do you really mean that no one should or could write about or speak about
a war because one has not stood on the battlefields? Were you serious when
you dictated that – really serious, now? Was Shakespeare at Actium or Phil-
lipi [*sic*]? Was G. B. Shaw in the boats with the French, or in the forts with
the British when St. Joan and Dunois made the attack that relieved Orleans?
And someone, I think, wrote a poem about Tir na nOg who never took a
header into the Land of Youth.

I have pondered in my heart your expression that 'the history of the world
must be reduced to wallpaper,' and I find in it only the pretentious bigness
of a pretentious phrase. I thank you out of mere politeness, but I must refuse
even to try to do it. That is exactly, in my opinion (there goes a cursed opinion
again), what most of the Abbey dramatists are trying to do – building up,

building up little worlds of wallpaper, and hiding striding life behind it all … It is all very well and very easy to say that 'the dramatic action must burn up the author's opinions.' The best way, and the only way, to do that is to burn up the author himself.

There are no little worlds of wallpaper in the tumultous theatre of O'Casey; a theatre of tragic violence and compensating laughter; a theatre of technical risks and fantastic visions. To this day *The Silver Tassie* remains an enigmatic challenge to many literary and theatrical interpreters, a work of revolutionary stagecraft so far ahead of its time that it has been treated as one of the brilliant failures of modern drama. Its ultimate fate belongs to the future. Nevertheless, there can be little doubt that the Abbey Theatre, which owed its very existence to the arrival of O'Casey – a fact that Yeats had acknowledged in his letter – should have accepted and produced his new play. Bernard Shaw wrote to O'Casey hailing him as a theatrical 'titan' and offered this eloquent praise of the play:

What *I* see is a deliberately unrealistic phantasmo-poetic first act, intensifying in exactly the same mode into a climax of war imagery in the second act, and then two acts of almost unbearable realism bringing down all the Voodoo war poetry with an ironic crash to earth in ruins.

Then in a letter to Lady Gregory, Shaw began by scolding her: 'Why do you and W.B.Y. treat O'Casey as a baby?' And he went on to attack Yeats for his failure to appreciate the play and the situation:

It is literally a hell of a play; but it will force its way on to the stage and Yeats should have submitted to it as a calamity imposed on him by an Act of God, if he could not welcome it as another *Juno* … But that is so like Yeats. Give him a job with which you feel sure he will play Bunthorne and he will astonish you with his unique cleverness and subtlety. Give him one that any second-rater could manage with credit and as likely as not he will make an appalling mess of it.

The play finally did force its way on to the stage a year later in 1929 when C. B. Cochran presented it in London, with a second-act war set designed by Augustus John, with Barry Fitzgerald as the comic Sylvester Heegan and the young Charles Laughton as Harry Heegan, the tragic football hero and crippled soldier who suffers for mankind. The production received mixed reviews but played to packed houses, though it had to close after two months due to excessively high operating costs. If O'Casey was stubbornly winning some of his artistic battles, he was gradually losing the economic war of survival, the long-range fight to go on writing his new plays on his own visionary terms. There was little money to be made from his concept of symbolic theatre. As an innovative playwright he was at least a generation ahead of his time, and he

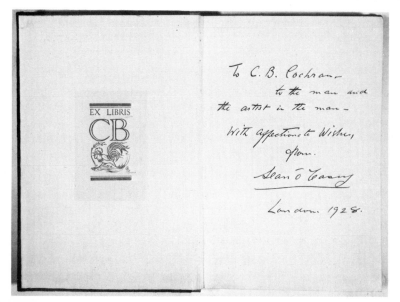

23rd Nov. 1929
AYOT ST LAWRENCE, WELWYN, HERTS.
STATION: WHEATHAMPSTEAD. L.&N.E.R. 2¼ MILES.
TELEGRAMS: BERNARD SHAW, CODICOTE.

4, WHITEHALL COURT, LONDON, S.W.1.

My dear Cochran

I really must congratulate you on The Tassie before it passes into the classical repertory. It is a magnificent play; and it was a magnificent gesture of yours to produce it. The Highbrows should have produced it: you, the Unpretentious Showman, DID, as you have done so many other noble and rash things on your Sundays. This, I think, will rank as the best of them.

I hope you have not lost too much by it, especially as I am quite sure you have done your best in that direction by doing the thing as extravagantly as possible. That is the worst of operating on your colossal scale: you haven't time to economize; and you lose the habit of thinking it worth while.

No matter! a famous achievement. There is a new drama rising from unplumbed depths to sweep the nice little bourgeois efforts of myself and my contemporaries into the dustbin; and your name will live as that of the man who didn't run away.

If only someone would build you a huge Woolworth theatre (all seats sixpence) to start with O'Casey and O'Neill, and no plays by men who had ever seen a five pound note before they were thirty or been inside a school after they were thirteen, you would be buried in Westminster Abbey.

Bravo!
G.B.S.
George Bernard Shaw

EX LIBRIS
CB

To C. B. Cochran —
to the man and
the artist in the man —
With affection & Wishes,
from.
Sean O'Casey
London. 1928.

Praise from Bernard Shaw to C. B. Cochran for the 'magnificent gesture' of putting on *The Silver Tassie* in London.

Sean, too, voiced his appreciation in a copy of the play which he inscribed to C. B. Cochran.

had to pay the price for his creative insight since the theatre of London was not ready for him and the theatre of Dublin had disowned him.

Four years later in 1933 when he finished his next experimental play, *Within the Gates*, a parable of life and death in the microcosmic world of Hyde Park, C. B. Cochran, who had lost money on his courageous production of *The Silver Tassie*, wrote to explain that he could not chance the risk of doing the new play, even though he admired it: 'You can't go on writing fine things, Sean, unless they bring some material reward. I suppose you are tired of people advising you to get back to the method of "Juno". I wish you would.' In the matter of sound business sense Cochran was justified in calling for a compromise between 'fine things' and 'material reward', but it was a compromise O'Casey was never prepared to make. And since he was to be confronted by the obvious advice of going back to the safe dramatic method of *Juno* throughout his life, his forthright reply to Cochran provides the best and only justification of his motives as man and artist: 'Your advice to go back to the genius of "Juno" might be good for me, but bad for my conception of drama.'

His conception of drama led to many lean years of sacrifice for him and his wife and three children, the first of whom, Breon, had been born in 1928 ten days after the rejection of *The Silver Tassie*. He was often in debt through the 1930s, and at one point in 1932, when he could no longer afford to live in London and had moved to a cottage in Chalfont St Giles, he wrote to the local Inspector of Taxes in a desperate and amusing attempt to explain his economic problem:

I now have only Twenty pounds in the whole world, but I send you as ordered Five pounds to keep the wolf from the door, leaving myself with Fifteen to keep myself, wife and kid, and help to promulgate the Gospel in foreign parts.

I appreciate your point that my debt to the Inland Revenue is now £236 odd, but it won't be higher on account of last year's income, for there was none, for which I cannot thank God. With your permission, I should like to make a point myself, and it is this: when we poor devils of Artists get anything, we get it all at once, and not regularly as others do, so that we have to pay more taxation than most persons. There seems to be a core of injustice in that.

In an effort to clear up this debt and placate a number of other creditors he was finally forced to sell part of the amateur rights of *Gunman*, *Juno* and *Plough* to the Samuel French Company for £300, though Bernard Shaw warned him not to do this: 'My advice is to let wife and child perish, and lay bricks for your last crust, sooner than part with an iota of your rights.' Shaw followed up his advice

Charlotte Shaw, photographed by GBS.

with a loan of £100, but it was not enough to prevent the unfortunate sale or keep the O'Caseys in black ink.

Charlotte Shaw, who was particularly fond of O'Casey, tried to take another approach to his problems. In a sympathetic letter of advice and comfort, she suggested that he should attempt to be more tractable in his relationships with people, and she added this poignant request: 'And oh! dear Sean, don't be too belligerent!' To which he responded, in something of an Elizabethan flourish, with his unique apology for his belligerence:

I don't know how much I must read into your advice 'not to be too belligerent'. God be my judge that I hate fighting. If I be damned for anything, I shall be damned for keeping the two-edged sword of thought tight in its scabbard when it should be searching the bowels of knaves and fools. I assure you I shrink from battle, and never advance into a fight unless I am driven into it.

James Joyce, like Sean, self-exiled and self-avenging.

It must be admitted that he was driven into it often, and with a seemingly paradoxical mixture of distaste and delight. He need not have had any fear of damnation on the grounds of cowardice, for his 'two-edged sword of thought' was seldom in its scabbard. The similarly half-blind and self-exiled Joyce, living out his years of wrath in Trieste, wrote out of a comparable rage for vindication when he aimed this profane prayer at his enemies:

O, Vague Something behind everything . . . Give me for Christ's sake a pen and an ink-bottle and some peace of mind, and then, by the crucified Jaysus, if I don't sharpen that little pen and dip it into fermented ink and write tiny little sentences about the people who betrayed me, send me to hell.

Even that seemingly remote and dark man, J. M. Synge, must be numbered among these self-avenging Irishmen who never forgot and seldom forgave, when one recalls the broadside 'The Curse' which, after the riot against his play at the Abbey, he addressed 'To a sister of an enemy of the author's who disapproved of "The Playboy"':

Lord, confound this surly sister,
Blight her brow with blotch and blister,
Cramp her larynx, lung, and liver,
In her guts a galling give her.

Let her live to earn her dinners
In Mountjoy with seedy sinners:
Lord, this judgement quickly bring,
And I'm your servant, J. M. Synge.

And so, amid such irreverent prayers and curses, the sword-searching O'Casey was in good company with his well-armed countrymen who, like the ancient Celtic bards, knew that sticks and stones could only break bones but sardonic words could break hearts. If O'Casey was sometimes too quick to counter-attack those critics who rejected his conception of drama, his fighting instinct was not a Quixotic pose. His opponents were real and powerful, even if they were not all knaves and fools, since they were formidable enough to keep his plays off the stage and prevent him from earning his living as a writer, and he could only strike back with the sword of his sharp words.

His sword was in action in October 1932 when he made public his angry refusal to accept the offer of membership in Yeats's newly formed Irish Academy of Letters, a refusal he shared with Joyce. In May 1933 he was in the field again when his short story, 'I Wanna

PROGRAMME.

THE ABBEY ROW.
NOT Edited by W. B. YEATS.

Another angry Irishman, J. M. Synge. This ingenious parody of an Abbey Theatre programme appeared at the time of the *Playboy* furore. The original and the skit are here seen side by side.

Saven Walters

Sean O'Casey

James Agate: 'facetiously erudite'.

Woman', which had been accepted for publication in Lady Rhondda's *Time and Tide*, had to be rejected when the printer refused to set the type for what he considered to be an 'immoral' work; and when it appeared in print a year later in his *Windfalls*, the Irish censorship board, not about to be outdone by a pious English printer, banned the book.

Then he was drawn into a battle on several fronts in February 1934 when James Agate, the influential dramatic critic of the *Sunday Times*, and Gordon Beckles of the *Daily Express*, wrote not only unfavourable but what he felt were insulting reviews of the London production of *Within the Gates*. The facetiously erudite Agate, sounding like a pontifical executioner who had somehow strayed out of Gilbert and Sullivan, peppered his brittle remarks with literary allusions and French phrases, and concluded that, according to the laws of Sainte-Beuve, *Within the Gates* was 'Beyond the

(*Opposite*) Sean in the late 1920s. 'I assure you I shrink from battle, and never advance into a fight unless I am driven into it.'

49

Agates': on the one hand it was 'obviously a work of art', and on the other hand it was obviously 'pretentious rubbish'. Obviously, therefore, his orotund effort to avoid offence only became more offensive when he set out to 'explain that "pretentious rubbish" is not nearly as offensive as it sounds. Grandeur of form may well go with vacuity of content, and it is the latter which makes the thing rubbish and the combination of the two which makes that rubbish pretentious. See Swinburne.' O'Casey replied to these pretentious remarks in a fifteen-hundred-word letter to the *Sunday Times*, but the editor, apparently anxious to protect the vulnerable Agate, printed only a third of it. The following examples from the letter indicate that O'Casey's strategy this time was to thrust the sword into Agate's heavy hands and allow him to prick himself with his contradictory edicts:

'O'Casey,' he says, 'is obviously incapable of thinking of any subject except in terms of art, and, obviously, "Within the Gates" is a work of art.' If obviously, how can the play be difficult; if it be a work of art how can it be rubbish? And, if O'Casey be incapable of thinking in a form other than a form of art, how can the play be pretentious?

'The appeal to the ear in the play,' he says, 'consists in the splendour of O'Casey's muscled prose.' A work of art, splendour of muscled prose, grandeur of form, and yet the thing is nothing more than pretentious rubbish!

'Not one word of the splendid chant in the beginning of the second act reached me.' How did Mr Agate know that the chant was splendid if he didnt hear a word of it? And even if he heard every word of it how could he call it splendid, if it was nothing but pretentious rubbish? See Swinburne again, I suppose.

In the manner of the traditional morality play, *Within the Gates* dramatizes the struggle between good and evil for the soul of a sinner, a Young Whore, the everywoman of the parable set in a Hyde Park world that reflects the spiritual and economic depression of the early 1930s. Like the Socialist Shaw, O'Casey insists that the failure of Capitalism was related to the failure of Christianity. But in his theatrical method he was exploring a new tradition in drama by constructing his four scenes or stylized tableaux in a cyclical configuration based on the four seasons, with realistic and fantastic characters and actions, with chanted songs and discordant music and group dancing, with what Brecht was to call the 'alienation' techniques of 'epic theatre', with what O'Casey himself described as the open and graphic form of cinema. In his autobiography he explained that he was trying to bring to the narrow confines of the naturalistic stage some of the 'geometrical and emotional' imagery of the film, a prophetic vision that cinema and theatre directors like Fellini and Bergman, Grotowski and Peter Brook, were to exploit a generation later. With appropriate irony Agate had inadvertently

Lillian Gish as the Young Whore
in the New York production of
Within the Gates, 1934.

and 'obviously' come close to the mark when he objected that the
play 'reads like "Alice in Wonderland" interleaved with Euclid!'

The theatrical innovations were astonishing in the originality and
vigour of their conception, but the salvation and damnation theme
was cast in a recognizable form that went back to medieval drama.
Therefore, when the incredulous Gordon Beckles objected that he
could not understand a word of it and wrote, 'I challenge Mr
O'Casey to tell the world what the play is *really* about,' O'Casey
found it impossible to resist the temptation to play with his dull
critic and replied with a comical but accurate swing of his sword:

Gordon Beckles challenges me to tell him what the play really means. My
mission in life is not to give Gordon Beckles a higher mind than he has,
for I am not a worker of miracles.

The New York theatre critic George Jean Nathan – a loyal and eloquent champion.

I always felt inclined to believe in the survival of the souls of animals, and now I know my belief to be well founded, for here we have an instance of the reincarnation of Balaam's ass, whose mouth no angel has yet opened.

Perhaps some compassionate angel decided that O'Casey had earned a brief respite from fighting. In a mood of great excitement he went to New York in September 1934 for a three-month visit to repair his shaky fortune, to oversee the American production of *Within the Gates*, which George Jean Nathan had arranged for him. His contact with Nathan went back to 1932 when the dramatic critic and editor began to print some of O'Casey's articles and first autobiographical sketches in his *American Spectator*. When the two men met for the first time in 1934, the sophisticated New Yorker and the rough-hewn Dubliner, they took to each other with the overwhelming attraction of colourful opposites and began a lifelong friendship. For a quarter of a century Nathan was a loyal and eloquent champion of O'Casey's works. In New York O'Casey also struck up a close friendship with one of his heroes, the playwright

Eugene O'Neill, and with the important dramatic critic of the *New York Times*, Brooks Atkinson.

Eugene O'Neill (*left*) and Brooks Atkinson of the *New York Times*.

The American visit was clearly one of the bright periods in his stormy life, for he fell in love with the warm-hearted country of Walt Whitman with its generous and extroverted people. But although he was now an established artist with an international reputation, and was treated with great respect and kindness, he was penniless when he arrived in New York wearing a new suit made from cloth given to him by Lady Astor, and with a £200 guarantee from Lady Londonderry in his pocket. The proud Irish proletarian had for once been forced to humble himself and accept the friendly help of two aristocratic English ladies. To complete the picture of his triumphal arrival in New York, Arthur and Barbara Gelb, in their impressive biography of Eugene O'Neill, provide the following details:

O'Casey, in his first (and only) trip to the United States, arrived in a brown suit and cap, bringing with him nothing but an extra set of underwear, a single shirt, a pair of socks and a sweater. He registered at the Royalton Hotel, where Nathan lived, and spent the first hours after his arrival testing all the electrical gadgets in his room and carefully distributing his few items of wardrobe among the drawers of his bureau.

In some amusing and humanizing ways, then, the fighting nonpareil was cast in a new role as the wide-eyed innocent, the country boy from dear dirty Dublin discovering the gadgets and wonders of the new world, and eventually, to his surprise and delight, the adulation of its people. He soon came into some modest rewards when his play, with Lillian Gish in the leading role, was fairly well received and ran for a respectable four months. The New York critics were divided in their praise and reservations about his courageous experiment, but there was no rancour in the lively disagreement, which only increased the public's desire to see the provocative work, and O'Casey emerged unscathed as a daring playwright of the future. If he was something of an unpredictable gambler in the theatre, he had taken the right risks.

He was also something of a celebrity now, and he was invited to Cambridge, Massachusetts, to give the Morris Gray Poetry Talk at Harvard University, where he spoke about the decline and fall of the naturalistic theatre. He was the guest speaker at a synagogue in New York where he addressed the congregation on the historical and cultural affinities of the Jewish and Irish people. He found sympathetic audiences for his ideas and curiosity about his works wherever he went, and in the years ahead it turned out that the main part of his uncertain income was to come from his American royalties.

By mid-December he had to end his highly successful visit and return to England where his wife was expecting their second child. And then the smoke of controversy appeared on the horizon again, for on 15 January 1935, the same day that his son Niall was born, the mayor of Boston, acting on the urgent advice of religious pressure groups, banned *Within the Gates*, which was about to start a tour of thirteen cities across the country after its lively New York run. The Rev. Terence L. Connolly, S.J., dramatic critic of the Jesuit magazine *America*, had appeared before the Boston censorship board and condemned the play as a danger to the faith and morals of the people: 'In spots it is unspeakable filth,' he declared, 'drenched with sex and written to point out the futility of religion.' This attack was supported by charges of 'blasphemy' and 'obscenity' by the Rev. Russell M. Sullivan, S.J., head of the Boston Legion of Decency, and Bishop Charles Wesley Burns of the Methodist Church, who was out of town at the time but allowed Father Sullivan to use his name in the protest to the mayor. Meanwhile a counter-protest in defence of the play was organized by a group of students and teachers from colleges in the Boston area – Harvard,

O'Casey the celebrity. This photograph illustrated an article on him by the columnist Joseph Alsop Jr in *Vanity Fair*.

Radcliffe, Wellesley, Tufts – many of whom had heard O'Casey's talk at Harvard or seen his play in New York, and they paraded to the mayor's office with a petition, urging him to remove his ban. Since O'Casey had unfortunately departed a month earlier, he joined his troops in spirit and rushed off a cable to America, part of which read:

THE BAN ON WITHIN THE GATES SHOWS THAT NOT THE PLAY
BUT THE PRIESTS ARE HOLDING THE CHURCH UP TO RIDICULE
STOP PLAY PUBLISHED YEAR AGO BUT NO PROTEST IN BOSTON
STOP WHY NO PROTEST WHILE I WAS IN THE CITY QUERY WHY
WAIT TILL I HAD GONE FROM THE CITY TO BAN PLAY AND BOOK
QUERY THEY NEGLECTED TO GIVE ME A CHANCE TO PERSONALLY
DEFEND THE WORK FROM THEIR ATTACKS STOP THIS IS THE
JESUIT AND WESLEYAN IDEA OF FAIRPLAY AND DECENCY STOP I
DONT WRITE PLAYS TO PLEASE PRIESTS STOP FATHER SULLIVAN
ASKS WHAT THE PLAY SYMBOLIZES STOP HIM AND HIS FRIENDS
OBVIOUSLY FOR ONE THING STOP PLAY EVIDENTLY STARTLED
THEM AS THE SACRING BELL DID THE CARDINAL WHEN THE
BROWN WENCH LAY KISSING IN HIS ARMS SEE SHAKESPEARE STOP

See Agate! But the mayor still said no, and the defenders of 'decency' in Boston won the fight. The tour of the play collapsed before it began, and there were to be no more royalty cheques for the O'Caseys.

Nevertheless, with the proceeds from the New York run of the play they were able to leave their frugal comfort at Chalfont St Giles and move back to London to a flat in Battersea. For a while O'Casey tried to earn some money by writing reviews, but it soon became apparent that according to the genteel spirit of the time he was temperamentally unsuited for this type of traditional puffery. In February 1935 he touched off a literary dispute in the *New Statesman and Nation* with his harsh review of *Love on the Dole*, the printed text of a popular play about the British working class by Ronald Gow, adapted from the novel by Walter Greenwood, which was enjoying a long run in the West End, and which O'Casey in his review had dismissed as containing too much patronizing propaganda and too little artistic merit. A flood of protesting letters appeared in the magazine, but the editor, Kingsley Martin, in the name of decorum, refused to print several of O'Casey's sharp replies. After waiting two months in censored silence for his moment of truth, O'Casey finally had an opportunity to take on all his opponents, including Martin, when Lady Rhondda invited him to write the guest-column, 'Notes on the Way', in the April 13th issue of her *Time and Tide*. He blasted them all and went on to stress his belief that the art of literary criticism in England was becoming a harmless game of polite and meaningless praise. Here are two characteristic examples from his column:

Most of the reviewers are mere polishers of brass, a job, even if well done, that wouldn't do much harm if we were made aware that the metal polished bright was brass; but the reviewers breathe on the brass, handle it fondly, and hold it up to the light as if they were polishing gold. If this should continue much longer, England may remain a land of hope, but she will cease to be a land of glory.

This ceaseless downpour of praise has left us all in such a soft and damp condition that when any author, critic, or clergyman gets a sudden and sharp prod of adverse criticism, he or she is breathless and, without a word of warning, throws a swoon. Many critics have a tendency, too, if one ventures to reply to them, of falling down in a dead faint, evidently thinking that their criticisms are written, not on desks or tables, but on the tops of holy altars.

Looking down from his editorial altar, Kingsley Martin promptly wrote a letter to the rival magazine, objecting that O'Casey had broken the rules of the game by using *Time and Tide* to attack the *New Statesman and Nation*. Martin also defended his refusal to print one of O'Casey's letters because 'it was extremely abusive', and if he were to reply in kind he would have 'merely written something about Irish guttersnipes and poltroonish attacks by papers that were only fit for the lavatory'. If this shameless abuse from an upright journalist who had himself invoked the gentlemanly rules against abuse were not proof enough that Martin had exposed his folly, O'Casey added the *coup de grâce* by sending a copy of the so-called

Kingsley Martin

Kingsley Martin, editor of the
New Statesman, whose editorial
attacks led to one of Sean's most
spirited (and successful) battles.

'abusive' letter to *Time and Tide*. It turned out to be one of the
least belligerent letters he had ever written in a fight, a firm and
coldly polite statement of his independent ideas. The whole incident, recorded in *The Letters of Sean O'Casey*, Vol. I (1975), was
an ironic reminder that a liberal British editor could be as insulting
and underhanded as some of the reactionary critics of O'Casey in
Boston or Dublin.

Apparently Yeats had followed the dispute and sympathized with
O'Casey to such an extent that it led to a significant reconciliation
between the two men. It was actually Yeats's friend Ethel Mannin
who inadvertently brought them together. Miss Mannin had joined
the protest against O'Casey's review, and in her letter to the *New*

Statesman and Nation on 16 February 1935 she scolded him severely because she thought he was sacrificing the proletariat for art:

Oh, to hell with the 'artist' as 'above the kings and princes of this world,' and 'above Labour Leaders and the Proletariat, too.' Art doesn't fill the empty belly, or pay the rent, or mend the kids' boots. Let Sean O'Casey go spouting that stuff on Clydeside or Tyneside or South Wales – and get a kick in the pants from the proletariat he considers not worth his artistic (*sic*) curse.

A strange rebuke to the noblest proletarian of them all! Miss Mannin failed to realize that he was not about to sacrifice his art or his proletarian loyalties; and she chose to misunderstand his point that the proletariat needed more than patronizing sympathy, that the proletariat should serve as the inspiration of good art rather than bad propaganda. And few knew better than O'Casey that empty bellies could no more be filled with propaganda than with art.

He was so distressed by this attack that a day after he read the letter he turned instinctively to a kindred artist and wrote warmly to the sad and ailing Yeats in Ireland – Yeats his old antagonist who had rejected *The Silver Tassie* because of what he considered its intrusive propaganda, Yeats with whom he now shared a common ground of artistic inviolability. Yeats was deeply moved by the gesture, and he wrote to Miss Mannin on March 4th to defend O'Casey and warn her about the bitter results of propaganda in art and life, and also to thank her for having provoked O'Casey into a mood of reconciliation:

I have had a friendly letter from O'Casey about my illness. He must have written it the day after he read your letter in the *New Statesman*. He is very emotional, and your attack, perhaps, made him lonely. Since we quarrelled with him years ago he has refused to speak to anybody belonging to the Abbey Theatre. Only two years ago he refused an invitation to lunch because he heard I was to be there. Though your defence of propaganda has had this admirable result do not let it come too much into your life. I have lived in the midst of it, I have been always a propagandist though I have kept it out of my poems and it will embitter your soul with hatred as it has mine.

Thereafter Yeats and O'Casey exchanged cordial letters, and when the poet came to London in May he invited O'Casey to dine with him and all was well between them. At this fortunate reunion they talked about their favourite Elizabethan poets and playwrights, about Communism and religion, and they made plans for a belated production of *The Silver Tassie* at the Abbey. Yeats had atoned for the tragic rejection, yet it really was too late to help O'Casey's career, since he had in the intervening seven years become known as the rejected playwright who wrote difficult and risky plays, a stigma that was to haunt him for the rest of his life.

Ethel Mannin, novelist and journalist. Her scolding led indirectly to Sean's reconciliation with the ageing Yeats.

Yeats at Rathfarnham in his sunset days. 'He is as big a fighter as ever,' wrote Sean, 'and will surely die with harness on his back.'

When the play was finally performed for the first time in Dublin on 12 August 1935, a predictable controversy broke out, though it was mainly confined to angry letters and public statements in the press. The Rev. M. H. Gaffney, a Dominican priest, and the playwright Brinsley Macnamara, now one of the Abbey directors, launched a virulent campaign against the play, O'Casey and Yeats. Macnamara resigned his post as director in a moral protest against the Abbey's decision to produce the 'obscene' and 'wantonly offensive' play; and Father Gaffney, in letters to the *Irish Press* and the Catholic *Standard*, issued a grave warning to Yeats:

The fracas over the *Playboy* was but a flash in the pan, a child's cracker, in comparison with the hostility with which the Abbey is confronted if it persists in defying Catholic principle and flouting that reticence which is characteristic of our people. Dublin people are not prudes or puritans if they exact from a government theatre a recognition and observance of the forms of plain etiquette. And plain etiquette will not tolerate horror, indecency or blasphemy, on or off the stage.

But Yeats stood by O'Casey this time and the play went on as scheduled, amid an uproar of verbal but no physical violence. The controversy was still hot when O'Casey and his wife arrived in Dublin in September for a two-week holiday, made possible by the earnings from his trip to America. Now O'Casey stood by Yeats and wrote a number of letters to the Irish papers in which he defended the poet as well as his play from the jaundiced views of Father Gaffney, Brinsley Macnamara and some of the unamused Irish reviewers. When several papers tried to create trouble by reporting

that the Abbey's decision to produce the rejected play was a re-
pudiation of Yeats, O'Casey was quick to point out the truth in
open letters to the Dublin and New York press: 'Mr. Yeats will
never be anything less than a great poet and a great man.' And
when he was back in London in October he commented on the
whole incident in a letter to George Jean Nathan:

I have been able only to think of you for some weeks past, for I took a
holiday that I had planned for five years, and went to see my own home town,
Dublin. A quiet holiday it was to be, spent meandering through many old
familiar places. I went, and, be God, I found myself in the midst of a fierce
and fiery battle! The Abbey had put on 'The Silver Tassie,' and all the critics
& some of the clergy were yelling and snapping & biting at everything they
saw or pretended to see in the play. The whole Free State tottered, & it
is tottering still. All the Irish critics & most of the Irish dramatists like to
get a welt at me; and, indeed, I sometimes return their welts with an ungrand
and a hundred thousand welcomes. At the moment the opposing forces are
withdrawing to their bases to prepare for a renewal of the fight whenever
the play goes on again. Many are determined to drive me body, soul, &
spirit out of Ireland, and they are using me as a lever with which to down
the Abbey. W. B. Yeats is an old man now, but he is as big a fighter as ever,
& will surely die with harness on his back. I enclose a few press-cuttings
to give you an idea of the kind of fight we are waging. Curiously enough,
I was met with a hail and hearty welcome everywhere I went – from worker,
priest, monk, & literary gent. except the critics. The fight, however, is a little
tiresome, & I don't think I'd join in were it not necessary to stand by Yeats.

No matter how tiresome the fight might be at times, he still
sounded like a man who never ceased to enjoy the sport as well as
the issue at stake in a contentious encounter. But he was genuinely
determined to stand by the man who should have been his bitter
enemy. The complex relationship between O'Casey and Yeats after
the rejection of *The Silver Tassie* in 1928 is full of human surprises.
In accord with his personal mythology, one might have expected
O'Casey to see himself as a proletarian St George girding himself
for battle against an autocratic dragon. His refusal to seek revenge,
however, tells us something about the fibre of his character. His
pride as well as his career had been hurt by the rejection, but he
avoided self-dramatization, he resorted to anger without vindictive-
ness. When his anger cooled he stated his case with considerable
restraint and fairness some years later in the fifth volume of his autobiography, *Rose and Crown*:

Yeats's denunciation of *The Silver Tassie* had done Sean's name a lot of
violence. The Nobel Prize winner, the Leader of English Literature, was a
judge against whom there was no appeal for the time being. Sean's flying
start had been rudely curtailed of its fair proportions, and he would have
to start over again, and fight the battle anew.

Significantly, then, instead of indulging in self-pity or planning a vendetta against Yeats, he set out to salvage his career by doing the one thing he felt he knew best, and he went on writing new plays for the theatre of the future on his own innovative terms. During the early 1930s a group of disgruntled writers in Dublin who were bitterly hostile to Yeats sought to recruit O'Casey to their cause of trying to undermine the name and influence of the poet, but he promptly told them what to do with their lost cause and gave them the back of his hand. He told them he would never stoop to that sort of wretched literary skirmishing.

O'Casey and Yeats met for the last time on the occasion of this Dublin visit in September 1935. It was to be O'Casey's first and last visit to his native land since 1926. The men met at the poet's house, Riversdale, in Rathfarnham, where they played croquet, a game that was alien to O'Casey. He had played hurling as a young man and would have been more effective with a hurley stick than with a croquet mallet. Needless to say, croquet was Yeats's game and he easily defeated O'Casey, who had never played before. As gamesmen or fighters, it would be very appropriate to imagine

'Riversdale', Yeats's Rathfarnham home, where Sean visited him for the last time.

O'Casey armed with a hurley stick and Yeats with a croquet mallet. But the fighters were on friendly terms now and they were able to refer to O'Casey's defeat at the Abbey Theatre seven years earlier without bitterness. Of course Yeats had been magnanimous enough to change his mind and produce *The Silver Tassie* at the Abbey a month before O'Casey arrived, in spite of a storm of critical and clerical protest. As a result of that vulgar protest the two men were drawn closer together by a common enemy, what Joyce had called the Irish rabblement. 'That was part of his greatness,' O'Casey had once said about Yeats, 'he hated the Irish crowd but he loved the Irish people.'

After they had put aside their croquet mallets, they talked about many things, but mainly about the stereotyped and stagnant situation at the Abbey. Yeats told O'Casey he realized that the theatre 'needed new life through a newer type of play', and he openly admired O'Casey's newest and most ambitious work: 'O'Casey, you've succeeded in your last play, *Within the Gates*. The co-ordination of mood, dialogue, and technique there is a success, where, I think, it is a failure in your *The Silver Tassie*.' Yeats had originally wanted to produce *Within the Gates* at the Abbey, but O'Casey felt that it would be too difficult to create the Hyde Park world in Dublin, and the Irish actors would probably have problems with the cockney idiom; so he insisted, no doubt with some degree of belated vindication, that it should be *The Silver Tassie*, and Yeats agreed. Looking back on that final visit with Yeats, in *Rose and Crown*, O'Casey alternately admired the poet's courageous defence of the artist and questioned what he called his aristocratic bias. 'There was no braver man among the men of Eireann than W. B. Yeats,' he wrote. 'In every fray of politics, in every fight for freedom in literature and art, in every effort to tempt Dublin's city into the lure of finer things, the voice of Yeats belled out a battlecry.' But with the limitations of what must be called his own proletarian bias, O'Casey also felt that Yeats was equally capable of retiring into that 'wallpaper world' which he had tried to impose upon O'Casey with the rejection of *The Silver Tassie*: 'The poet had played with his toys too long. Aristocratic toys, self-fashioned; a few coloured with a wild philosophy, all tinged with beauty, some even with a gracious grandeur; but he had played with them all too long.' No doubt O'Casey also felt that croquet mallets were aristocratic toys. Then, in an amusing and unlikely speculation, he wrote: 'Born into the proletariat, Yeats would have made a magnificent docker.' Fortunately, the world that gladly lost a magnificent docker gained a magnificent poet; and on this O'Casey agreed.

When Yeats died on 28 January 1939, Lennox Robinson decided to edit a 'W. B. Yeats Commemoration Number' of *The Arrow*, an occasional magazine of the Abbey Theatre. Robinson asked O'Casey to contribute an article but he refused, feeling disinclined to write on the spur of the moment. Nevertheless, he did begin to shape his impressions of Yeats, and by the end of the year they appeared in an article, 'Literature in Ireland', which was published in the December 1939 issue of the Moscow English-language magazine, *International Literature*. Apparently he was making a significant point in his choice of magazine, for he decided to tell the Russians and the world about Yeats, rather than the back-biting Irish who had often attacked the poet throughout his lifetime. In this article, which was reprinted posthumously in *Blasts and Benedictions* in 1967, O'Casey presented an introduction to Irish politics, culture and literature. He stated that Joyce was the greatest novelist and Yeats the greatest poet in the English language, but again he qualified his great praise by making a distinction between Yeats the universal artist and Yeats the man who set himself apart from the common people:

The greatest of these big figures was, undoubtedly, Yeats, the strange, dreamy, faraway poet, who could, all in a moment, be so practical in the affairs of the theatre. He is the great poet of the period, and so far, possibly (to me, certainly), the greatest poet writing in the English language. At the first go-off, and, indeed, for some time, Yeats built all, or almost all, his poetry on the legends and romances that sparkle in the literature of the Gaelic past, though, to no little extent, he fled too far away from the common people, turning the poet into a cold aristocrat who turned his head up to the heavens, looking at no one below the altitude of a star; failing to see that many, especially among the workers, were themselves, in their own way, seeking a vision, more roughly, perhaps, but no less deep than his own.

But having made this point about Yeats's aristocratic bias and visionary aloofness, O'Casey went on to exalt the poet as a courageous fighter. And he disclosed that in their final meeting Yeats had expressed his growing awareness of the needs of the common people:

Yeats, too, was a fine and fearless fighter, raising himself against the intimidation, the stupid intolerance, the ignorant opposition of the religious societies, anxious to make sure that nothing outside of their own seedy, senseless, and lackalight lumber should be said or sung in the land.

   In the last years of his life, Yeats became much more human, drew nearer to the world's needs, and, as he told me himself, became intensely interested in the new voice of the resurgent working-class speaking in its own way, and demanding the earth and the fullness thereof. He is gone now, and Ireland will miss him sorely, for he was Ireland's greatest poet, and a great warrior to boot.

For all this magnanimous praise, it took a few more years before O'Casey was able to overcome his proletarian bias and at last make

Jim Larkin: bronze head by
Mina Carney. Larkin and Yeats,
in Sean's view, were two of
Ireland's greatest fighters.

his peace with the formidable wraith of Yeats. In 1946 he wrote an essay on Yeats called 'Ireland's Silvery Shadow', in which he composed a lyrical tribute of unqualified devotion to the man who had deprived him of a theatre for his plays. This little-known piece, also reprinted in *Blasts and Benedictions*, thanks to the fine editorial efforts of Ronald Ayling, was originally written for the BBC Spanish Service and was broadcast on the radio in a Spanish translation. This time it was more likely economic necessity rather than eccentric choice that prompted O'Casey to use such an unusual medium for his views, since, ironically, it was due to Yeats's rejection of *The Silver Tassie* and the subsequent decline of O'Casey's income that he had to seek such out-of-the-way commissions in order to earn his living. In this broadcast essay he celebrated Yeats's 'strange and magnificent genius' by comparing him to Ireland's 'uncrowned king', Parnell, and placing him among Lady Gregory's 'Gods and Fighting-men' – no Irishman 'bore a tougher shield, a brighter sword, or a loftier crest, than W. B. Yeats, the poet'. This was the highest possible praise, which until this time O'Casey had only bestowed upon Dublin's promethean labour leader, Jim Larkin. But even in the full flush of this myth-making mood, O'Casey characteristically brought the god-like Yeats down to earth by giving him his fair share of human frailties: 'arrogant at times, not always wise; but vigorous, poetic, and of unbreakable integrity'. O'Casey could have been describing himself as well as Yeats in these intractable terms.

Finally he addressed himself directly to the charge which he along with many others had levelled at Yeats, that he often assumed the detached pose of a lofty dreamer. He recalled one of Yeats's early poems, 'Fergus and the Druid', in which King Fergus, tired and dissatisfied with the life of action, makes a bargain with a druid to exchange his kingdom for a miraculous bag of dreams. The king is now transformed into a poet, but in taking upon himself the druid's poetic insight he has also become grey-haired and hollow-cheeked. Nevertheless, Fergus willingly accepts the consequences of the bargain, saying to the druid:

> *A wild and foolish labourer is a king*
> *To do and do and do, and never dream.*

O'Casey used a pre-1925 edition of Yeats's poems which contains this early version of the poem. In later editions, however, Yeats revised and improved the lines to read:

> *A king is but a foolish labourer*
> *Who wastes his blood to be another's dream.*

Although O'Casey had a copy of the revised lines, he apparently felt that the early version was more explicitly relevant to his intense concern about the alternatives of *doing* and *dreaming*, action *vs.* art in Yeats's life and work, and also in his own. Yeats had often tried to reconcile the inevitable conflict that arises between the life of action and the life of art, symbolically in his Cuchulain plays, especially *At the Hawk's Well*, and more directly in a poem like 'The Choice':

> The intellect of man is forced to choose
> Perfection of the life, or of the work,
> And if it take the second must refuse
> A heavenly mansion, raging in the dark.
> When all that story's finished, what's the news?
> In luck or out the toil has left its mark:
> That old perplexity an empty purse,
> Or the day's vanity, the night's remorse.

The world-weary Fergus had no regrets about the night's remorse and chose to rage in the dark by readily abandoning his kingdom for the druidic gift of dreams. O'Casey, who was himself confronted by Fergus's choice throughout his lifetime, saw in Yeats a greater Fergus, a poet who had managed to perfect his life as well as his art:

Yeats, dreaming his life away, did and did as heartily as any king.... This strange man, seeking the excitement of supernatural knowledge, and, in his visionary life, casting but a careless thought or two on the practical things which concern the movements of man's mortal existence: this man probing himself into the mystery of the why and wherefore of what man called life; loving the dream far more than the thing to do, or the thing done; yet spent far more of his life in doing things than in dreaming about them.

As concrete evidence O'Casey then drew up an impressive catalogue of 'the amazing number of active things that this man crowded into his dreaming life': his founding and shaping of the Abbey Theatre with Lady Gregory; his share in the development of a new style of acting and new scenic design; his search for and encouragement of new playwrights; his vigorous defence of his theatre and its controversial playwrights from constant attacks by the Irish puritans and patriots; his writing and editing of a magazine in which he expressed his uncompromising ideas of theatre and art; his share in the fight for Ireland's claim to the Hugh Lane pictures; his notable participation in political issues as a member of the Irish Senate; and many more militant deeds in the practical world.

This was O'Casey's final testament to Yeats, the practical dreamer, and it may be fair to say he had done full justice to the man who had been somewhat less than just to him on one crucial occasion. In O'Casey's mind Yeats had outdone King Fergus by matching his lofty dreams with noble deeds. But the essay and the issue were not finished yet, for O'Casey was also determined to measure himself against the choice that confronted Fergus. As a man who had chosen self-exile from his native land, as an artist who had placed his work above all practical considerations, O'Casey realized that his deeds had to be confined to his writing, to the dreams he might express through the power of his pen. He had withdrawn from the controversial arena of Irish life and art, and even though he remained vitally concerned about the literary and political struggles, he had chosen to be a distant spectator. But if like Fergus he had willingly chosen to rage in the dark, he also insisted, as Yeats had always done, that there had to be light in the darkness. Perhaps because he felt he had to compensate for his own limited catalogue of practical deeds, he included in his essay an eloquent defence of the life of art, even going so far as to claim that ultimately the *dreaming* was superior to the *doing*, though the two should complement each other:

To do and never to dream is worse than to dream but never to do; for to dream and never to do is to at least live in a rich state, even though it be an unnatural condition to striving humanity; but to do, and never to dream, is to humiliate that humanity into insignificance, and to dishonour the colour and form in that arrangement of things by God which man calls life.

This high praise of the druidic gift of dreams should not come as too great a surprise, for there can be no doubt that while he was a militant socialist committed to political and revolutionary action, O'Casey also lived and wrote in a rich state of dreams. It must have been the militant dreamer in him who urged Lady Gregory 'to fight on for that which is above & before all governments & parties – Art & Literature which are the mantle & mirror of the Holy Ghost, and the sword of the Spirit'. He defended the more modest and practical dreams of the tenement mothers in his early plays; and he celebrated the more lyrical and fantastic dreams of the crafty peasants in his later plays. For all these characters it must be said that, in the spirit of Yeats's epigraph from an Old Play, 'In dreams begins responsibility.' Dreamers all, and many of them superb clowns with the rare wisdom of fools, in their eccentric ways they are determined not to humiliate humanity. O'Casey often insisted he was an atheist, but he also insisted, in an article on *Within the Gates*, that 'The first Dreamer is the Holy Ghost.'

The Holy Ghost was his metaphor of ultimate truth, and as if to make certain that no one could accuse him of using it as a dreamer's weapon reserved for Irish targets, he also examined many aspects of British life and art in relation to the great dream or truth. Early in 1936, for example, when the Shirley Society of St Catherine's College, Cambridge, invited him to give an informal talk, he spoke on the subject, 'The Holy Ghost Leaves England'. He warned the university audience that the liberating energy of the Holy Ghost would surely abandon the country unless Englishmen had the courage to dream of a better and richer life, and to fulfil the dream through revolutionary actions, instead of remaining entrenched in the smug deceits of their conventional British ways.

Throughout 1936 he published a number of articles on the English theatre in *Time and Tide* – some of them were rejected when Lady Rhondda found them too provocative – in which he attacked the commercial theatre of the West End for its cheap standards; and in calling for the artistic independence of a National Theatre his lone voice once more turned out to be a generation ahead of his time. With more courage than prudence he concentrated his assault on reigning critics and playwrights like James Agate and Noël Coward, because he believed they were partly responsible for the mediocrity of the English theatre, for he reasoned that audiences conditioned to the conventional charades of Coward and his brittle imitators, most of them blessed by the critical imprimatur of the pontifical Agate, would be incapable of appreciating the superior and innovative works of O'Neill and Pirandello, let alone those of O'Casey, and would therefore fail to realize the ultimate need for the higher idealism of a National Theatre.

One might argue persuasively that O'Casey was right on all these counts. And in the process one might also discover that his continuing dilemma arose largely from the stubborn fact that he was too often too right; he was so very intemperate and accurate in his sword-swinging battles that he usually succeeded in alienating as well as out-scoring his influential opponents. When he decided to collect his articles on the deficiencies of the English theatre for a book, *The Flying Wasp*, his publisher and personal friend Harold Macmillan, with the best of intentions, urged him to try to be less 'combative' in his writing. To which O'Casey, in a letter of 25 September 1936, replied in his most characteristic stance: 'Everything I have written, up to the present, has been "combative," and the sword I have swung so long is now stuck to my hand, and I can't let go.' Macmillan also counselled him to omit a chapter in which he criticized the critics, and to remove some of the unmannerly sting from the whole manuscript, for a man of his stature in the theatre should avoid 'brawling in church', all of which inspired the following unassailable response from O'Casey:

Why should I leave out an article in reply to a criticism of my own work? My works are, at least, additions to the drama, and defending them, I defend the drama. Am I to leave it out because 'it is not done,' or because it is not 'good form'? I hope I know something about good manners, but on a question of principle, good form can go to the devil. Invariably, I have done the

Harold Macmillan, Sean's friend and publisher.

The

FLYING WASP

A LAUGHING LOOK-OVER OF WHAT HAS
BEEN SAID ABOUT THE THINGS OF THE
THEATRE BY THE ENGLISH DRAMATIC
CRITICS, WITH MANY MERRY AND AMUS-
ING COMMENTS THEREON, WITH SOME
SHREWD REMARKS BY THE AUTHOR ON
THE WISE, DELICIOUS, AND DIGNIFIED
TENDENCIES IN THE THEATRE OF TO-DAY

by

SEAN O'CASEY

There is a nest of wasps that must be
smoked out because it is doing the
theatre infinite harm. MR. J. AGATE.

LONDON
MACMILLAN & CO. LTD.
1937

Title-page of *The Flying Wasp*,
1937.

things that are not done, and left undone the things that are done, and I amnt much the worse for it. The theatre is more than good manners. As for 'brawling in church,' well, Jesus Christ did it before me, and I occasionally follow in His steps.

By the time the book was published in 1937 O'Casey had already moved on to other battlefields, for he was in his own unorthodox way following in the steps of Karl Marx as well as Jesus Christ. His eclectic and unpredictable belief in Communism was more emotional than political, more of a personal faith than a party programme, though it was deeply rooted in his early working-class experiences in Dublin and his contact with the Socialist Jim Larkin. He liked to use lessons from Scripture to support his Communist faith, which in simple yet basic terms was a creed founded on good deeds. He often assured his friends in Ireland, England and America – and no doubt amused them by it – that since they accepted the belief that they were their brothers' keepers they must be unconscious Communists. He must have confounded his dear friend George Jean Nathan, that elegant man of the world, when in a letter of 28 October 1936 he made this proclamation:

To me the great proletarian dramatist of America is the bould O'Neill. And the great proletarian critic is – G. J. N. For, my dear George you are a red. You may say you dont give a damn about this or that, but you are a red revolutionary in the theatre, and you always have been one – at least since I began to know you, and that's twelve years ago. You want the best that can be given to the art of the theatre, and that is the creed of the communist.

A year later on 24 November 1937 he wrote to Bernard Shaw about the new Communist play he was writing, *The Star Turns Red*, in which the Star of Bethlehem is transformed into the Red Star. And he urged Shaw to write a play about the rebellion of Jack Cade: 'You could make a Communist St. Joan of him.'

There were of course times when he carried his loyalty to Communism to unwarranted extremes. From March to June 1938, in articles and letters, he was involved in a bitter dispute with Malcolm Muggeridge over the Moscow treason trials. The Soviet govern-

Malcolm Muggeridge.

ment could do no wrong in O'Casey's myopic eyes and he defended the star-chamber trials which led to the execution of Bukharin, Zinoviev, Radek and others. When Muggeridge attacked the trials O'Casey attacked Muggeridge, for O'Casey was suspicious of all anti-Communists and automatically exposed them to the devastating scorn he reserved for enemies of the Russian revolution, the proletarian struggle to which he remained idealistically and uncompromisingly loyal throughout his life. The right-wing *Daily Telegraph*, in which Muggeridge's article had originally appeared, refused to print O'Casey's reply, so he promptly sent it to the left-wing *Daily Worker*, and thereafter the fight overflowed into the columns of several other papers with new participants. The Socialist Emrys Hughes, in whose *Forward* some of the battle was fought, was probably right in describing O'Casey as 'a sentimental and emotional communist'; and O'Casey was probably right in justifying his emotional defence of Russia on the grounds that the British press 'fears Russia as the devil is said to fear holy water'. But perhaps O'Casey best understood his combative shortcomings when he confessed in a letter to Nathan on 27 March 1938: 'I am altogether too vehement to be a good critic. I can't keep calm.'

In spite of these shortcomings, however, taken at the top of his eloquent and humanistic form, he was a compassionate Communist full of brotherly love for all mankind. Possibly the bould O'Casey had much in common with that earthy and visionary figure, Pope John XXIII, for the revolutionary Communist Sean shared with his namesake the revolutionary Catholic John a fundamental faith in the goodness of men of all creeds. This comparison will no doubt distress orthodox Catholics and Communists, but it would most likely have delighted and amused both men. When the ecumenical Pope was featured as 'Man of the Year' in *Time* magazine on 4 January 1963, he was characterized in the following comment:

Everywhere, John has always made a point of meeting and fraternizing with non-Catholics and 'anyone who does not call himself a Christian but who really is so because he does good.'

When the ecumenical O'Casey was asked in the summer of 1963 to explain his concept of Communism, he echoed precisely the Pope's views in a comment which indicates that the great humanity of both men – men for all years – ran deeper than any religious or party labels:

Every man who puts his best effort into his life and work, be he a doctor or a bricklayer, is a communist whether he knows it or not, for he's helping to improve the common good and making the world a better place for himself and his family and his country, and all the countries of the world.

A further instance of O'Casey's attempt to embrace all mankind, to link the Communist, Christian and Persian faiths, all faiths, really, can be found in the letter he wrote to the *New Statesman and Nation* on 2 August 1941, protesting against the suppression of the *Daily Worker*. Herbert Morrison, the Home Secretary and Minister for Home Security, had banned the Communist paper as a threat to the war effort, but O'Casey argued that the paper was making a valuable contribution by trying to bring about a friendly relationship between England and the Soviet Union; and one passage in the letter, an eloquent plea for freedom of the press and the people, might well be called O'Casey's Communist Manifesto:

Of course, Communists have to deal with other things beside literature – with bread, for instance; but Christ dealt with that: the bread is given, right enough, but we don't get it – we have to fight for it. There is a Persian proverb which says: 'If you have two pennies, with one buy bread, and with the other a lily.' But if we have but one penny, we can buy only bread. It has been my fight for a long span of years now to try to bring about a condition in which the worker spending his penny on bread will have one left to buy a lily.

That dedicated struggle for bread and the lily accurately describes one of the prevailing themes in O'Casey's later plays and his monumental autobiography. He had been working on what he called his 'curious autobiography' since 1936, and the first volume, *I Knock at the Door*, which covered the first ten years of his life, appeared in 1939. During the next fifteen years he expanded the story in five more volumes, each covering roughly a decade, except

Spine for book – '*Knock at the Door*'

For the first volume of his autobiography, *I Knock at the Door*, Sean sketched his ideas for the jacket design.

(*Overleaf*) Sean the compassionate Communist and John the revolutionary Catholic shared – if nothing else – a fundamental faith in the goodness of all men.

71

A caricature done for the
magazine *Courier* in 1964.

for the last one which dealt with two decades. Since he chose a semi-fictional form for his saga, he ignored the type of straight information one usually expects to find in an autobiography, vital statistics and dates. He was more concerned with the imaginative reality of his world and the impressionistic shaping of his mind and faith through the years of childhood, adolescence and maturity. The following outline provides an approximate chronology for each volume: *I Knock at the Door* (1939), 1880–1890; *Pictures in the Hallway* (1942), 1891–1904; *Drums Under the Windows* (1945), 1905–1916; *Inishfallen, Fare Thee Well* (1949), 1916–1926; *Rose and Crown* (1952), 1926–1934; *Sunset and Evening Star* (1954), 1934–1953.

By using the third-person narrative approach of the novel and a *persona* to represent himself – first the young Johnny Casside, later the grown up Sean – he was able to see himself from an aesthetic distance and avoid the limited personal pronoun. Together with this narrative method he relied upon the multiple focus of the drama for many episodes that are rendered almost entirely in dialogue. There is a rich profusion of dramatic voices which represent real and imaginary characters in Dublin and London, New York and Devon. The freedom and virtuosity with which he develops his narrative and dramatic techniques, mixing and even superimposing them in some scenes where he combines tragedy and comedy, fantasy and farce, allows him to use a variety of styles and moods. His language can be terse and concrete, discursive and digressive, poignant and lyrical, satiric and ironic, burlesque and profane, inflated and oracular, colloquial and exalted. Like the voluble characters in his plays, O'Casey can be profligate and exuberant with words, playing with their sounds and meanings, indulging in the Joycean game of puns, parodies, malapropisms and comic invective.

Joyce and O'Casey were proud, lonely and paradoxical figures, injured men with a magnificent rage for life who had to leave Ireland in order to be completely Irish; yet as artists they remained courageous Dubliners who recreated the conscience of their city in relation to the hope of mankind. Dublin often disappointed them, but in the final reckoning it served them as faithfully as they served it. The last word of *Ulysses* is 'Yes', the last word of the autobiography is 'Hurrah!'

At one point in *Sunset and Evening Star* O'Casey says, 'Come, let's thump the world with talk.' And that is what he has done in a glorious way through the six volumes that make up over half a million words. In a work of such magnitude it is to be expected that the words may clog the pages from time to time with rhetorical excesses, with fretful grievances and needless alarums, especially in the later volumes where the narrative sometimes runs down as he lingers too long in polemics. But on the whole the words do make a wonderful thump. In all these eloquent and contentious respects the work follows in the tradition of George Moore's three-volume autobiographical masterpiece, *Hail and Farewell*, to which it bears a striking resemblance. Furthermore, the powerful figure of Shaw emerges as one of O'Casey's special heroes, and at one point in *Sunset and Evening Star* he might well have been describing himself when he wrote the following testament to the memory of Shaw:

Bernard Shaw – one of Sean's special heroes.

The earth was his home, and he loved it. He was at home among the mortals. His epiphany was the showing forth of man to man. Man must be his own saviour; man must be his own god. Man must learn, not by prayer, but by experience. Advice from God was within ourselves and nowhere else. Social sense and social development was the fulfilment of the law and the prophets. A happy people made happy by themselves. There is no other name given among men by which we can be saved, but by the mighty name of man.

For O'Casey, then, as for Shaw, the divine spirit, the life-force is within man; God is the guardian but man is the measure of his own destiny. When the first volume of the autobiography appeared in 1939, however, O'Casey's spiritual destiny may have been assured but his financial destiny was in grave doubt. Since the rejection of *The Silver Tassie* every play he wrote had to wait for uncertain production after it had been published, and he was to write sixteen more plays under this condition, eight full-length and eight short or one-act plays. There was to be a long wait for royalty cheques and they were small when they dribbled in. The little he earned went mostly towards the education of his children – Breon was eleven, Niall was four, and Shivaun was born in 1939 – for in 1938, on the advice of Shaw, he had moved out of London to the little village of Totnes in Devon, where the children could attend a progressive and creative school, Dartington Hall.

Through the 1940s and '50s the main source of his income was the well-received autobiography, and some critics even suggested that as an unproduced playwright his reputation might ultimately and ironically rest upon the epic autobiography. But such was far from the case at the start when *I Knock at the Door* was originally greeted with some brickbats. Oliver St John Gogarty, his friend of earlier years, attacked the book in a review in the *Observer* on 12 March 1939, attributing its failure in large part to his notion that 'O'Casey has, after all, a grudge against Life'. O'Casey counter-attacked with one of his sword-swinging letters, which the timorous editor of the *Observer* refused to publish, in which he replied: 'On the contrary, I love Life. But I have more than one "grudge" against the futilities, shames, stupidities, and romantic nonsense that distort and maim Life.' Then two months later, as if to confirm his protest against the follies of life, the Irish censorship board, in a futile and shameful grudge against O'Casey, banned the book.

Meanwhile he went on writing his extravagant and provocative plays. Early in 1939 he finished what is probably his most overtly political play, *The Star Turns Red*, which was published a year later by Macmillan in London, though the firm's New York office rejected it because of its Communist theme. In order to get it produced O'Casey had to give the play to an amateur company, the left-wing Unity Theatre, which performed it in London in March

1940 with two alternating casts. James Agate, who had been stung on several previous occasions by O'Casey's pen, possibly took the precaution of overstating his review in the *Sunday Times* on 17 March and declared the play to be 'A Masterpiece', not for its hortatory Communism but for 'the passion, pathos, humour, and, above all, poetry with which this great play is hung':

I came away impressed above all by a verbal splendour which can throw away: 'Where's his "Workers of the world, unite!" now? Hid in the dust of his mouth and lost in the still pool of his darken'd eyes!' upon a minor character. Shakespeare's prodigality again, which could give the 'lated traveller' jewel to a First Murderer. Now, at last, Mr. O'Casey has achieved that towards which in 'The Silver Tassie' and 'Within the Gates' he was feeling his way.

Agate's high praise may have been excessive, nevertheless the play undoubtedly projects a theatrical and poetic excitement that is not entirely diminished by the melodramatic conflict between Communist and Fascist stereotypes. The action takes place during a strike that resembles the 1913 Dublin General Strike, even to the point of presenting one character, a labour leader named Red Jim, who is clearly modelled after Jim Larkin.

Even before *The Star Turns Red* was performed O'Casey had already finished his next play, *Purple Dust*, which was published in November 1940. Once again he had moved in a new direction with yet another theatrical challenge, as if he were beginning a new career at sixty. *Purple Dust* was the first of his comic fantasies, a merry extravaganza in the mock-pastoral convention which was to be the dominant form, with many ingenious variations, of all his remaining plays. In his early tragicomedies he had used an anti-heroic structure to mock the national excesses and yet affirm his faith in the Irish people. In the moralities of his middle period he had used the expressionistic form of non-realistic symbolism to expose the spiritual and social disorder in the larger world beyond Ireland. Now, in his late comedies, like a mellow and enchanted Prospero who was to go on writing into his eighties, he turned to the fantastic and satirical tradition of pastoral entertainment to present his comic vision of the world as it might be. Besides *Purple Dust*, these versions of pastoral include *Red Roses For Me* (1942), *Oak Leaves and Lavender* (1946), *Cock-a-Doodle Dandy* (1949), *The Bishop's Bonfire* (1955), *The Drums of Father Ned* (1960).

Purple Dust is a high-spirited satire of pastoral affectations in which two bumbling Englishmen in search of an idyllic past are defeated by a group of crafty Irish peasants. If it bears something of a resemblance to Shaw's *John Bull's Other Island*, it also reflects O'Casey's other island in a state of merry Celtic mischief. Unfortunately, however, no play that ridiculed the English was likely to be

Sam Wanamaker, with the author beside him, rehearses *Purple Dust* for its London production in 1953.

performed during the Second World War when England was fighting for its very existence. After a delay of five years the play was finally produced in 1945 by the Liverpool Old Vic company. Eleven years later, in 1956, it was performed in New York with great success by an off-Broadway company at the Cherry Lane Theatre and ran for just over a year, the longest run ever for an O'Casey play.

Red Roses For Me, one of his most autobiographical and lyrical works, a mythic poem for the theatre, was first performed in Dublin at the Olympia Theatre in 1943, the first Irish premiere of an O'Casey play in seventeen years. *Oak Leaves and Lavender*, in which he turned from ridicule to celebration of the ancient traditions of England, as well as paying homage to the Battle of Britain, was produced by Bronson Albery at the Lyric Theatre in Hammersmith in 1947. With a sly reference to Yeats, O'Casey sub-titled this play 'A Warld on Wallpaper,' though it is much more than that with its masque-like Prelude and Epilogue and dancing spirits, its anti-Fascist rhetoric, its curious mixture of Cornish and Irish comedy.

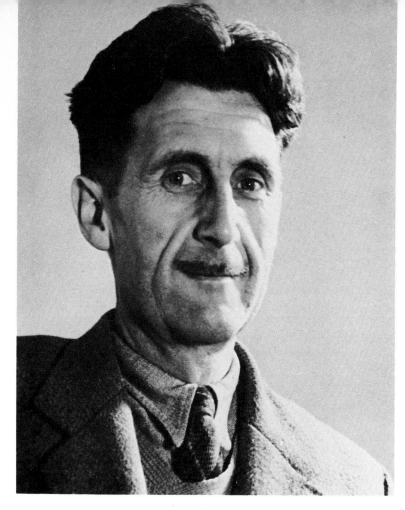

George Orwell. His review of *Drums Under the Window* complained of 'blatant Irish nationalism' – as the pot complained of the kettle's blackness.

Through the years the autobiographical volumes were receiving a generally popular reception, particularly in America, though there was some rough weather in 1942 when the Irish censorship board banned *Pictures in the Hallway*. The next volume, *Drums Under The Windows*, was dismissed by George Orwell, in a rather nasty review in the *Observer* on 28 October 1945, as a vulgar example of blatant Irish nationalism, even though it should have been abundantly clear that O'Casey consistently disaffiliated himself from and mocked his excessively nationalistic countrymen. Ironically and unaccountably Orwell himself sounded more like a vulgar example of blatant British nationalism as he wrapped himself in the Union Jack and objected to the 'special status enjoyed' by Irishmen in England; objected specifically to some lines of Irish patriotic poetry O'Casey had quoted; objected to the numerous references to Cathleen ni Houlihan; and demanded to know why the British should tolerate someone like O'Casey. 'Why is it that the worst extremes of jingoism and racialism have to be tolerated when they come from an Irishman?' Once again the upright editor of the *Observer* refused to print O'Casey's sharp reply – a copy was sent to Orwell who decided to ignore it – in which he had little difficulty illustrating that it was precisely the type of arrogant jingoism and racialism that Orwell was practising which denied any special status let alone enjoyment for Irishmen in England. O'Casey also caught Orwell napping by pointing out that the lines of 'Irish' patriotic verse were actually taken from Tennyson's 'Maud'! So much for 'maudern English literary criticism', he concluded, but not before he read Orwell a brief lesson on the history of Cathleen ni Houlihan: Mr Orwell was 'seemingly unaware that this is a name for Ireland ... that the name Cathleen ni Houlihan was forced upon us by Mr Orwell's England, who, for many centuries, made it a penal thing to write down the name of the country, so her poets were forced to adopt the allegorical ones, one of which so annoys the reviewer.'

While Orwell was attacking O'Casey for his excessive Irish nationalism, O'Casey was busy in his autobiography, his plays and his letters, attacking the Irish for their excessive nationalism and religiosity, both of which created the climate of literary censorship and contributed to his exile from his native land. In a letter to Nathan on 8 February 1944 he wrote: 'Ireland is becoming more virulent than ever over my books, "a venomous expatriate" is the latest. The whole of Ireland's becoming a Boston, a Boston without any Americans.' In a letter to William Rust on 11 September 1944 he wrote: 'Eire is, of course, now little more than an enlarged sacristy, with Christ outside and all the doors locked.' And around this time, in a letter on censorship to an official of the Irish Civil Liberties organization, he stated: 'In Ireland they wear the fig leaf on the mouth.'

When the fourth volume of the autobiography appeared in 1949, *Inishfallen, Fare Thee Well*, in which O'Casey charted his disenchantment with Ireland, most of the Irish reviewers condemned the book as bitterly anti-Catholic as well as insultingly anti-Irish. And again there were numerous objections to O'Casey's big bow-wow rhetoric. The distinguished English critic Desmond MacCarthy, however, in his review in the *Sunday Times* on 30 January 1949, had considerable praise for the book, and he made some significant observations on the rhetorical and religious arguments. On the first issue he scored the following point:

O'Casey is a tremendous rhetorician. Personally I love the superb but today despised Art of Rhetoric; and I can forgive O'Casey even when he continues intoxicated with his own, even after I have recovered my sobriety; I wait patiently for the phrase which will be final and quick as a blow – and I am seldom disappointed.

On O'Casey's attitude toward Catholicism, MacCarthy appeared to be playing Cranly to O'Casey's Stephen Dedalus, perhaps remembering that in Joyce's *A Portrait of the Artist as a Young Man*, Cranly, the ironic confidant and confessor, had remarked to the disenchanted and rebellious Stephen: 'It is a curious thing, do you know, how your mind is supersaturated with the religion in which you say you disbelieve.' O'Casey had never been a Catholic, and yet his life was in curious ways coloured and saturated with Catholicism; his grandfather was a Catholic, he grew up in the most Catholic city in the world where all his closest friends were Catholic, he married a Catholic and his children were baptized Catholics, and he probably understood the faith better than most Catholics; so there may well be some measure of ironic Cranly-truth in the latter part of this comment by MacCarthy:

O'Casey is possessed with a loathing of the Church of Rome and any religion as 'the opium of the people,' the instrument of the upper class. Yet his imagination, and his moral judgements, too, are saturated in Catholicism.

And yet this was not the whole truth, especially the statement about his 'loathing of the Church of Rome', as O'Casey himself pointed out in a confessional letter to MacCarthy on 7 February 1949. He wrote to thank MacCarthy for his favourable review but primarily to insist that he was anti-clerical not anti-Catholic; that he had never attacked the dogma of the Church; and that while he disbelieved in the faith he could never loathe the power and the glory of its lovely mythology. Neither Joyce nor his Stephen could have gone as far as O'Casey went in this moving *odi et amo* expression of disbelief and adoration:

I don't really loathe the Roman Catholic Church. That is a wide term, embracing all the souls baptised into its communion, and even those baptised outside of it. The cardinals and bishops form but a tiny part of it. I loathe those who are turning her liturgy into vulgar nonsense and her temples into dens of thieves. Dante said this about the famous monastery of Monte Cassino – that the monks had turned the place of St. Benedict into a den of thieves. No intelligent man could possibly loathe the dogmas embedded in the 'deposit of faith left by the apostles.' The idea of the Incarnation, the ascent, the coming of the paraclete, and all the moral philosophy, the poetic tales connected with these, are beautiful; and, though not accepted either in substance or in fact, remain beautiful, and I am not one to loathe the lovely.

His last three full-length comedies, *Cock-a-Doodle Dandy*, *The Bishop's Bonfire* and *The Drums of Father Ned*, should be considered in the light of his remarks to MacCarthy, for these works abound in that satirical disbelief and fantastic adoration which make O'Casey such a profoundly rebellious and religious playwright.

The O'Casey family: Sean,
Eileen, Niall, Shivaun and Breon.

82

A scene from *Cock-a-Doodle Dandy* at the Edinburgh Festival, 1959. The Sergeant and One-Eyed Larry discuss what kind of a bird it was that carried off the priest.

(*Opposite*) The Messenger leads the Cock out of Marthraun's house.

His scepticism arises out of his disillusionment, his feeling that the organized Churches have failed to help man achieve the good life in this world. His adoration arises from his idealism, his unwavering faith in the potential power and glory of God's greatest handiwork, man. The three plays are pastoral celebrations in which the forces of clerical repression and bourgeois folly are comically exposed by the youthful and mythic forces of freedom and joy. In *Cock-a-Doodle Dandy*, one of O'Casey's favourite works, the wild festivities are presided over by the apolcalyptic figure of an enchanted Cock, a merry Lord of Misrule in the form of a man-sized dancing creature out of the beast-fable tradition. The mythic Cock, with his Aesopian shrewdness, Dionysian spirit and Celtic magic, with his beautiful young women as allies, and the aid of such folk figures as Robin Adair and Maid Marion, leads the fight for freedom in the Irish village of Nyadnanave, which in Gaelic means Nest of Saints, but with O'Casey's ironic pun also becomes a Nest of Knaves.

Variations on the theme of Nyadnanavery are played out with some darker implications in *The Bishop's Bonfire*, with some more exuberant implications in *The Drums of Father Ned*. In both plays the title characters, Bishop Mullarky and Father Ned, like Godot, never appear, but like bad angels and good angels they are active in the wings; the bourgeois Bishop as the instigator of a book-burning bonfire to wipe out the source of temptation, the rustic Ned as a Catholic priest with a Protestant drum who prepares to lead an ecumenical Tostal or festival in honour of God and man. O'Casey had lost little of his gift for comedy and prophecy in these plays, as can be seen in the following examples. Two of the pastoral clowns in *The Bishop's Bonfire* are the Prodical, a 'paycock' of an intemperate Protestant who is always making and breaking vows of abstinence, and his 'joxerian' friend Rankin, a pious Catholic who is seldom without fear of sin. In one scene when the men are confronted by the temptation of drink, Rankin utters his dire warnings and the Prodical defends the freedom of his soul with a comic flourish:

RANKIN *(plaintively to Prodical)*.   Your good angel's trying to pull you back, Prodical; but if you once get to the keg, you're cornered! It's an occasion of sin, an' may do immortal harm to your poor soul!

PRODICAL *(coming over to Rankin and thrusting his face upwards towards Rankin – indignantly)*.   Looka, me good angel, I won't have you hoverin' over me soul like a saygull over a fish too deep for a dive down! I'm not goin' to let foreign bodies write down messages on me soul the way a body writes down things on a Christmas card. Me soul's me own particular compendium. Me soul's me own spiritual property, complete an' entire, verbatim in all its concernment.

Now turning from comic freedom to joyous prophecy, the young people in *The Drums of Father Ned* are preparing for Father Ned's rites of spring with a carnival of song and dance when Nora McGilligan has to defend the Tostal in honour of Angus the Young, the Celtic god of love, with his harp and bright singing birds. She insists that there is no conflict between the Pagan and Christian ideals of joy, that the Blessed Lord represented more than thou-shalt-nots and would have been pleased to see His people dancing in Ireland:

If He didn't dance Himself, He must have watched the people at it, and, maybe, clapped His hands when they did it well. He must have often listened to the people singin', and been caught up with the rhythm of the gentle harp and psalter, and His feet may have tapped the ground along with the gayer sthrokes of the tabor and the sound of the cymbals tinkling.

This rhythmic vision of the Blessed Lord with His tapping feet was almost performed in Dublin in 1958. The Archbishop of Dublin, however, acting as if he were one of the dour and unrhythmic clerics in the play, was distressed by the prospect of O'Casey drumming and dancing in his city. His publicly announced displeasure led to the indirect banning of *The Drums of Father Ned*, which of course he had not read, and which had been scheduled to open at the Dublin International Theatre Festival as part of the 1958 Tostal. Originally the works of three outstanding Irish writers were to be performed, O'Casey's Tostal play for a Tostal, a dramatization of Joyce's *Ulysses*, and three mime plays by Samuel Beckett. But when in the announcement of his disapproval the Archbishop let it be known that he refused to open the Theatre Festival with the usual celebration of the Mass, as had been the custom in previous years, the Tostal committee lost its nerve and all the plays were dropped. A member of the Dublin Council of Irish Unions, which threatened to boycott the Festival if the plays were performed, acted as if he as well as the Archbishop were a character in the play when he announced at a meeting that 'if the clergy took objection to the production of these plays, they would be quite safe in stepping behind the clergy. If they disregarded the advice of the clergy, they were lost.' With such ironic accuracy life imitates art in Dublin.

A month after this controversy, in March 1958, the unofficial ban of O'Casey's collection of essays, *The Green Crow*, was mysteriously lifted by the Irish Customs Office, which had seized all copies of the book and prohibited its sale in Ireland for a year. Outraged by the whole matter of Irish censorship, O'Casey decided to issue an edict of his own from Devon, and he banned all professional productions of his plays in Ireland, a prohibition he stubbornly maintained for seven years until 1964, when he relented shortly before his death. But laughter is a more effective weapon than prohibition, and in one chapter of his banned book, 'The Power of Laughter: Weapon Against Evil', he wrote this appropriate prayer:

We couldn't live without comedy. Let us pray: Oh, Lord, give us a sense of humour with courage to manifest it forth, so that we may laugh to shame the pomps, the vanities, the sense of self-importance of the Big Fellows that the world sometimes sends among us, and who try to take our peace away. Amen.

Nevertheless, prayer and laughter could not hold back the advance of old age and the septuagenarian O'Casey had many infirmities to endure. By the 1950s he had practically lost the sight in his left eye, and his 'good' eye, with its chronically ulcerated cornea, was fading. Every day of his life he had to sponge his eyes with water as hot as he could bear in order to wash away the suppurating fluid that burned his eye-sockets and temporarily blotted out his vision. He was subject to regular attacks of bronchitis which

weakened his heart, and in 1956 he had to fight his way back from two major operations within two months, kidney and prostate, only to have his heart broken at the end of the year when his twenty-one-year-old son Niall died suddenly of leukemia. He was a long time recovering from that shock, and later he recorded his grief in an elegiac essay in his son's memory, 'Under a Greenwood Tree He Died', which appeared in *Under a Coloured Cap* (1963). Like his Mrs Tancred and Juno Boyle, it was now his turn to *caoine* or lament the tragic death of a dear young son:

To go so young, and life so much within you and around you. Oh, where was the Lord's deliverance?

> He delivered Daniel from de lion's den,
> Jonah from de belly of de whale,
> The Hebrew chillun from de fiery furnace;

but he never delivered you. God wanted him, and it pleased him to take the boy, says a voice from Ireland. Oh, God, oh, Ireland! We wanted him to stay far more than God wanted him to go. He was needed and so God called him away, said another voice – from Ireland. God must be hoarse calling to heaven all the young lads and girls who die far before their time. . . .
I cry a caoine for my Niall, for though I may bear it like a man, I must also feel it like a man, and cannot feel ashamed that my sigh will be in the winds that blow where'er his dear ashes blow, for he had very gentle, loving ways within him; but the caoine, as he would wish, goes out for all the golden lads and girls whose lovely rose of youth hath perished in its bud.

In spite of his intense sorrow he never succumbed to despair, and he went on trying to write hopefully about life in everything he touched, for example in his final plays, three short satiric comedies, *Behind the Green Curtains*, *Figuro in the Night*, *The Moon Shines on Kylenamoe*; in 'The Green Crow Caws' and 'Immanuel', in *Under a Coloured Cap*, two powerful statements of humanistic faith by a laughing yea-sayer in his eighties. But he could hardly be blamed if he wasn't always optimistic about the human condition, for he was a man of extremes who could damn as well as bless with his eloquent pen. A representative selection of these two opposing aspects of his nature can be found in the appropriately titled *Blasts and Benedictions*, a volume containing some of his non-dramatic writings from 1926 to 1964, on subjects ranging from literature to politics to religion to people. Ronald Ayling took the felicitous title from a review O'Casey wrote of a volume of Bernard Shaw's letters, in which he stated: 'What a man Bernard Shaw was for sending his blasts and benedictions everywhere, falling over the land like the thistledown from a blown-out dandelion.' Obviously the same was true of O'Casey, though he was a more controversial figure than Shaw and therefore became more notorious for his blasts

Niall O'Casey. 'To go so young, and life so much within you ...'

Well into his eighties, Sean was
still writing, still tapping out his
blasts and benedictions on his
ancient typewriter.

than his benedictions. In one article, written in 1963, he attributes his penchant for blasting to his rough experiences in Ireland during the first half of his life: 'I have lived a troublesome life in Ireland, in my youth hard times in the body, and in my manhood years a hard time in the spirit. Hardship in my young days taught me how to fight hard, for if that characteristic wasn't developed then, it meant that one became either a slave or a lickspittle.' He became such a hardened and uncompromising fighter after surviving his first forty-six years in Dublin that he concluded: 'Indeed, had I been Adam, I think I should have resisted the angel with his sword of flaming fire that drove him and his Eve from the Garden of Eden.'

This is a devastatingly honest self-portrait. Nevertheless, some softer touches must be added to complete the picture, for this intractable Celtic Adam was also capable of bestowing his benedictions over a wide range of interests, though he sometimes damned one thing in order to bless another. As early as the 1930s he was blasting the commercial West End theatre and prophetically calling for a National Theatre in England that might lead to 'greater things for the glory of God and the honour of the English theatre'. He became enthusiastic over an early play which D. H. Lawrence had written at the age of twenty-one, *A Collier's Friday Night*, and he condemned the English theatre and its insensitive managers for their failure to support such works of exceptional artistic promise: 'Had Lawrence got the encouragement the play called for and deserved, England might have had a great dramatist.' He demonstrated the wide range of his wrath on various occasions by blasting British socialists, Russian Communists, and Irish Catholics for their indifference to the power and glory of art and literature. He read earthy sermons on the joy of sex to puritanical Christians: 'And we should remember that God made us from the waist down as well as from the waist up.' He identified Ireland's fanatically austere patron Saint as the cause of medieval Ireland's failure to develop a native Gaelic drama:

I am inclined to believe that it was neither the lack of roads, nor even numerous calls to battle, but the invasion of Ireland by St Patrick that ended any hope of an Irish drama, till enough centuries had passed to allow of evolving the liberal mind ready and independent to produce it.

He saved his unqualified benedictions for his favourite writers: Joyce and Yeats, Shakespeare and Boucicault, Synge and Lady Gregory, Brian Merriman and Charles Lever, Ibsen and Shaw, Strindberg and Chekhov, Gorki and O'Neill, Whitman and Mayakovsky. Among contemporary playwrights he singled out John Arden, about whom he wrote, with a blessing for Arden and a blast for the critics who were slow to recognize his talent:

Indeed, it seems to me that Arden's *Serjeant Musgrave's Dance* is far and away the finest play of the present day, full of power, protest, and frantic compassion, notwithstanding that, on its first presentation, it was scowled and scooted from the theatre by most of our intelligent and unintelligent drama critics.

Waiting for Godot at the Arts Theatre. 'I am not waiting for Godot to bring me life . . .'

He let fly some qualified blasts at Arnold Wesker's Centre 42 plan, set up to bring art to the masses, because he felt that the working people should participate directly in their own theatre, learning to write and act and produce their own plays, rather than being exposed to the cultural charity of performances by transient theatre companies. And there were qualified blasts for *Waiting For Godot*, for while he recognized the genius of Samuel Beckett he rejected the play's decadence and pessimism:

Beckett? I have nothing to do with Beckett. He isn't in me; nor am I in him. I am not waiting for Godot to bring me life; I am out after life myself,

even at the age I've reached [seventy-six]. What have any of you to do with Godot? There is more life than Godot can give in the life of the least of us. That Beckett is a clever writer, and that he has written a rotting and remarkable play, there can be no doubt; but his philosophy isn't my philosophy, for within him there is no hazard of hope; no desire for it; nothing in it but a lust for despair, and a crying of woe, not in a wilderness, but in a garden.

Throughout his career, from 1926 to 1963, he had directed a volley of blasts at the critics who tried to tell him how to write his plays, critical and clerical reviewers in Dublin, London, and Boston, who had accused him of writing plays that were too provocative or too profane; plays in which he had supposedly committed a multitude of sins under the unholy trinity of immorality, blasphemy and obscenity. He was therefore not defending the orthodox views of the middle-class establishment when in August 1964, only a month before he died, he wrote his final manifesto in the form of a special blast at the Theatre of the Absurd in an article slyly called 'The Bald Primaqueera'. In this effort he boldly attacked Artaud, Ionesco and Pinter, as well as their imitators, Rudkin, Simpson and Orton, because of their often gratuitous preoccupation with cruelty and violence, their easy preference for theatrical tricks rather than rich dramatic language, and their denigration of the human body. On this last point O'Casey was especially vehement:

To them the body is a vile body, and it is nothing more. The Christian Church nourished and nursed this idea, aiming at getting out of the body to be present with the Lord. The idea didn't work and it doesn't work now – except among a lot of playwrights, busy making the mind worse than the body. . . . These peering, leering playwrights have no natural or supernatural licence to jeer at these essential bodily practices. None of them is the mental or physical outcome of an immaculate conception. Each has a mortal button on his belly.

Thus, at the age of eighty-four, and indeed throughout the last decades of his life when he suffered chronically from a variety of painful and near fatal ailments, O'Casey, like the poet he admired so much, Walt Whitman, remained a bardic celebrant of the mortal and palpable human body. He often declared that the greatest glory of the body was represented in 'the soft thighs of a young woman'. He was against censorship of the body as well as the mind, and the handsome young women of his later plays, in contrast to the courageous mothers of his early works, are emblems of the beautifully mortal body and the quickening dance of love. His young women are sisters to Yeats's Crazy Jane and Joyce's Molly Bloom – Yeats and Joyce and O'Casey, three randy old pagans from puritan Ireland celebrating the glory of sex with a rage of delight in their women of the golden thighs.

(*Opposite*) Sean at eighty-one.

There are those occasions, however, when O'Casey forsakes the rich-grained earthiness of Joyce and Yeats in order to pursue an idealistic impulse, and at such times his sentimental benedictions reveal a soft spot in his imagination. For example, in an epilogue to 'The Bald Primaqueera' he offers a final blessing for heroic women in an attempt to counteract what he thought was the poisoned view of life and love in the Theatre of the Absurd. He had heard two news stories on the wireless, one about a fifteen-year-old girl who had lost her life saving a ten-year-old boy from drowning; the other about a policewoman who had risked her life to rescue a baby from the arms of its insane father threatening to jump with it from a roof. His reaction to these incidents, in contrast to his reaction to incidents of violence in the Theatre of the Absurd, provoked the following benediction and blast:

Brave woman, brave teen-ager lass. Ah, to hell with the loutish lust of the Primaqueera. There are still many red threads of courage, many golden threads of nobility woven into the tingling fibres of our common humanity.

In the name of that common humanity, it must be granted that praise for this kind of heroism is commendable. How could it be otherwise? Nevertheless, what is involved here is an emotional reaction to life, not art. Such acts of pure heroism are important, but they are a matter for secular hagiography, not dramatic literature. Nor, one suspects, will it really further the cause of drama to oppose the Theatre of the Absurd with a Theatre of the Brave. Furthermore, those 'red threads of courage' and 'golden threads of nobility' – unfortunately O'Casey had a tendency to lapse into such purple phrases from time to time – must be interwoven with the darker threads of irony and the motley threads of comedy when the raw incidents of life are used in the fabric of art. As a playwright who had followed this complex method of transmuting experience into art in all his plays, O'Casey must have known this; but as a man responding to an emotional experience in life, he could not resist the temptation to embroider his feelings with sentimental language.

He often drifted into a somewhat similar mood when he wrote about the Soviet Union, a country for which he had maintained an unbroken loyalty since the Revolution. He seldom blasted the Russians because of his idealistic view of Communism, and because he felt he might be giving aid and comfort to the capitalist enemies. On some occasions, however, he did scold the Russians for their puritanism and their party-line adherence to 'socialist realism', as, for example, in an article he wrote for a Soviet magazine in 1960, where he stated:

This is me. ←

Por Pussy

This is me too. →

3 Months ago.   at Present.

We have a pussy that we got as a
little kitten 3 months ago, & you can
imagine how it has grown by these pictures.
                                        Sean

Through the years when the theatre was denied him, Sean reached his private audience through letters – hundreds of them – to young and old. Some, like this one to a small girl, were illustrated in his own quirky style.

to him – most of them had apparently discovered a trusting and compassionate voice in his works – they wrote in friendship, they confessed their problems to him, they asked for his advice, they named their children after him, they argued with him, they praised him, they identified themselves with his alienation and his aspiration. And he responded with painstaking generosity and an open heart.

In the summer of 1956, for example, a New York housewife wrote to him about her inconsolable despair. She explained that her father had once worked with the great American Socialist leader, Eugene V. Debs, and she felt there was no longer any hope for social progress because the ideals of Debs and Jim Larkin had been forsaken. She now found it impossible to go on living a hard and lonely life without hope, with a sickly son and recent death in her family. The half-blind ailing O'Casey, who was still recovering from two operations, and who six months later was to lose his son, took up his pen and tried to comfort the despondent stranger with a letter that characteristically and indelibly illustrates the power and the glory of O'Casey:

My dear Mary,

It is not for me to say nay to your sad letter; but surely it is the lot of all of us to know the feverish brow, and the body hot with illness, or cold with the many hopes vanished, a voice lost, & no light, apparently, before us. Only apparently, for the light is there always, tho' we often keep our eyes shut so that we cannot see. I am aware of all you say about underpaid workers, of many a funeral; thro' many strikes, I have eaten dry bread & bitter waters,

99

with my half-famished comrades; but never lost the will to keep fighting. Ireland misses Larkin just as the USA misses Debs, for such flames are rarely kindled; but they, in the work of others, will flame again, if not in America or Ireland, then somewhere else to lighten & warm the whole family of man.

I know what a housewife has to face & has to do. I've scrubbed bare floors – no oil cloth for the poorer slums – kindled poor fires, washed my own & my mother's poor shirt & shift; but it was no treadmill task to do what we could to keep ourselves alive, & go about; at least, dishonestly clean; for no tenement dweller could keep honestly clean under the conditions, around, about & above them. I did chores before I became ill, to help my wife; & am beginning again – washing up, peeling spuds, carrying down the garbage, etc. It is partly good for us, for it is routine, & this checks the excitement of the mind, & gives us a rest. We cannot always suffer ecstasy. There must always be a lot of 'petty service', if not for others, then for ourselves. Each has to go thro' the routine of petty life day by day, year in & year out; there is no escape, nor should there be, for we are civilized animals that must accept civilization's laws.

I wish I could write you a long letter, but I'm still away from normal activity, & soon grow tired.

You have my sympathy, and a faraway touch of a hand that wishes you well, and (your son) Michael, too. I still have the same view of life; I love it, even in the midst of pain, when the candle of activity gutters. Shake Michael's hand for me, and give me your own.

Sean O'Casey

By the summer of 1964 the candle of his life was guttering, but its low flame burned brightly until the end. In August he suffered a heart attack and had to spend two restless weeks in the Torbay Clinic. He was eager to be at home with his wife and his writing. His home was now in a suburb of Torquay. Ten years earlier, when they were forced out of their house in Totnes by their landlord, the O'Caseys had moved into a flat in St Marychurch, Torquay. Now their Torquay landlord had died and the house of flats was soon to be sold, which meant that the unfortunate prospect of another move hung over them through that final summer. His wife was alarmed at the thought of what moving to a strange new place might mean for her failing husband. Besides his heart condition, his eyesight was practically gone. At the beginning of the year the doctor had declared he was blind, though somehow, mysteriously, he managed to see feelingly, he went on writing, playing with words, scribbling notes for manuscripts, touch-typing his letters in an unbroken routine day by day.

'He knows the exact distances of everything in the house,' his wife said, 'and when people see him moving about so freely and confidently they don't realize that like a blind person he does it all by memory and instinct.' She was afraid that if they had to move

41 Trimlands Road, St Marychurch, Torquay – the O'Caseys' last home.

Sean with Barry Fitzgerald, the original Fluther Good in *The Plough and the Stars* at the Abbey Theatre. This happy reunion after long separation was occasioned by the making of a documentary film, *Cradle of Genius*, on the Abbey.

to a strange place he would go crashing into the furniture, become demoralized and collapse. In the end it was not his eyes but his heart that brought him down. As his good friend Brooks Atkinson wrote in a moving tribute: 'In eighty-four years of unselfish living it was the first time that his heart had failed him.'

After his second heart attack he had died peacefully in his sleep with his wife at his side on 18 September. His body was cremated four days later and his ashes were scattered in the same place that his son's ashes had been scattered seven years earlier, in the Garden of Remembrance at the Golders Green Crematorium in London, in an area between the Shelley and Tennyson rose beds. What he had written about his son Niall could now be offered as a fitting memorial to Sean himself:

He had gone the way he had lived – as a flame of serious vitality, gaiety, and glee. He is now a handful of dust scattered over a Garden of Remembrance.

1880 30 March, born at 85 Upper Dorset Street, Dublin, to Michael and Susan Casey.
28 July, baptized John Casey at St Mary's Church, Church of Ireland.

1886 6 September, father Michael dies at age forty-nine.

1895 Acts the role of Father Dolan, the patriotic priest in Dion Boucicault's *The Shaughraun* at the old Mechanics Theatre in Abbey Street, which nine years later is rebuilt as the Abbey Theatre.

1900 Teaches Sunday School at St Barnabas Church, North Wall, Dublin.

1903 Works as a common labourer on the Great Northern Railway of Ireland.

1906 Learns the Irish language, joins the Drumcondra Branch of the Gaelic League, and gaelicizes his name to Sean O'Cathasaigh.

1907 Joins the St Laurence O'Toole Club and writes his first stories and articles for the Club's manuscript *Journal*, which was read at meetings.
25 May, first publication, an article, 'Sound the Loud Trumpet', in *The Peasant and Irish Ireland*.

1910 Founder-member and secretary of the St Laurence O'Toole Pipers' Band.

1911 Joins Jim Larkin's Irish Transport and General Workers' Union.

1913 Secretary of the Wolfe Tone Memorial Committee; secretary of the Women and Children's Relief Fund during the Dublin general strike and lock-out.

1914 6 February, brother Tom Casey dies at age forty-four. March, secretary of Irish Citizen Army.

1917 25 November, acts in the St Laurence O'Toole Dramatic Club's production of Thomas K. Moylan's *Naboclish* at the Empire Theatre, now the Olympia.

1918 1 January, sister Isabella Casey Beaver dies at age fifty-two.
Publications under the name Sean O'Cathasaigh: *The Story of Thomas Ashe; The Sacrifice of Thomas Ashe; Songs of the Wren No. 1; Songs of the Wren No. 2; More Wren Songs.*
9 November, mother Susan dies at age eighty-one.

1919 Publication of *The Story of the Irish Citizen Army.*

1920 Abbey Theatre rejects his first two plays, *The Harvest Festival* and *The Frost in the Flower.*

1922 15 April, Abbey Theatre rejects *The Seamless Coat of Kathleen.*
28 September, Abbey Theatre rejects *The Crimson in the Tri-colour.*
17 November, Abbey Theatre accepts *The Shadow of a Gunman.*

1923 12 April, *The Shadow of a Gunman* opens at the Abbey Theatre.
1 October, *Cathleen Listens In* opens at the Abbey Theatre.

1924 3 March, *Juno and the Paycock* opens at the Abbey Theatre.
7 June, his first visit to Lady Gregory's home at Coole Park, Galway.
29 September, *Nannie's Night Out* opens at the Abbey Theatre.

1926 8 February, *The Plough and the Stars* opens at the Abbey Theatre.
10 February, Irish nationalists riot in the Abbey Theatre against *The Plough and the Stars.*
23 March, goes to London to receive the Hawthornden Prize of £100 for *Juno and the Paycock.*
May, has his portrait painted by Augustus John.

1927 23 September, marries Eileen Reynolds Carey in the Roman Catholic Church of All Souls and the Redeemer, Chelsea.

1928 January, moves to 19 Woronzow Road, St John's Wood.
20 April, Abbey Theatre rejects *The Silver Tassie.*
30 April, birth of his son Breon.

1929 11 October, *The Silver Tassie* opens in London at the Apollo Theatre.

1930 22 September, film of *Juno and the Paycock*, directed by Alfred Hitchcock, is released.
10 November, film of *Juno and the Paycock* is burned in the street in Limerick by Irish nationalists.

1931   October, moves to Hillcrest, Chalfont St Giles, Bucks. November, writes his first autobiographical sketch, 'A Child is Born,' which later becomes the opening chapter of *I Knock at the Door*.

1932   July, writes *A Pound on Demand*, a one-act play.

1933   May, his short story, 'I Wanna Woman', is censored by the printer of *Time and Tide*.

1934   7 February, *Within the Gates* opens in London at the Royalty Theatre.
13 September, leaves Southampton on the *Majestic* and arrives in New York on 19 September for American première of *Within the Gates*.
October, publication of *Windfalls*, a collection of early poems, four short stories, and two one-act plays.
22 October, *Within the Gates* opens in New York at the National Theatre.
16 November, gives the Morris Gray Poetry Talk at Harvard University on 'The Old Drama and the New'.
4 December, *Windfalls* is banned by the Irish Censorship of Publications Board.
12 December, leaves New York on the *Britannic* and arrives in Liverpool on 23 December.

1935   15 January, birth of his son Niall.
15 January, *Within the Gates* is banned by the Mayor of Boston, forcing the cancellation of a scheduled tour of thirteen cities.

12 August, *The Silver Tassie* opens at the Abbey Theatre. September, returns to Dublin for the last time on a two-week visit and meets Yeats on friendly terms.

1936   February, gives a talk, 'The Holy Ghost Leaves England', to the Shirley Society of St Catherine's College, Cambridge.

1937   8 February, *The End of the Beginning*, a one-act play, opens at the Abbey Theatre. March, publication of *The Flying Wasp*, a collection of essays, articles and reviews.
15 March, film of *The Plough and the Stars*, directed by John Ford, is released.

1938   September, moves to Tingrith, Totnes, Devon.

1939   March, publication of *I Knock at the Door*, first volume of the autobiography.
16 May, *I Knock at the Door* is banned by the Irish Censorship of Publications Board.
28 September, birth of his daughter Shivaun.

1940   12 March, *The Star Turns Red* opens in London at the Unity Theatre.
10 June, becomes a member of the new Advisory Board of the London *Daily Worker*.

1942   March, publication of *Pictures in the Hallway*, second volume of the autobiography.
16 December, *Pictures in the Hallway* is banned by the Irish Censorship of Publications Board.

1943   15 March, *Red Roses For Me* opens in Dublin at the Olympia Theatre, directed by Shelah Richards.

1945   17 January, turns down an offer of up to $100,000 to write the scenario for a Hollywood film of Thomas Wolfe's *Look Homeward, Angel*.
October, publication of *Drums Under the Windows*, third volume of the autobiography.
31 October, *Purple Dust* opens in Liverpool at the Playhouse, performed by the Liverpool Old Vic company.

1946   26 February, *Red Roses For Me* opens in London at the Embassy Theatre, presented by Bronson Albery.

1947   11 January, his brother Michael Casey dies in Dublin at age eighty-one.
30 January, his friend Jim Larkin, the Irish labour leader, dies in Dublin at age sixty-nine.
13 May, *Oak Leaves and Lavender* opens in London at the Lyric Theatre, Hammersmith, presented by Bronson Albery.
16 December, the Irish Censorship of Publications Board removes the ban against *I Knock at the Door* and *Pictures in the Hallway*.

1949   January, publication of *Inishfallen, Fare Thee Well*, fourth volume of the autobiography.
10 December, *Cock-a-Doodle Dandy* opens in Newcastle-upon-Tyne, produced by the People's Theatre.

1950   30 January, *Cock-a-Doodle Dandy* opens in Dallas, Texas, at the Arena Theatre, directed by Margo Jones, the American première.

1951   25 April, *Red Roses For Me* opens in Houston, Texas, at the Playhouse, directed by John O'Shaughnessy, the American première.
18 July, the Abbey Theatre in Dublin is heavily damaged by fire several hours after the performance of a revival of *The Plough and the Stars*.

1952   July, publication of *Rose and Crown*, fifth volume of the autobiography.

1953   20 June, *The Silver Tassie* is performed in Berlin in a German translation by Elizabeth Freundlich, directed by Fritz Kortner, accompanied by a riot in the theatre, partly an attack against O'Casey and his play, partly an anti-semitic attack against Kortner's return to the Berlin theatre.

1954   9 June, moves to 3 Villa Rosa Flats, 40 Trumlands Road, St Marychurch, Torquay, Devon.
July, publication of *Sunset and Evening Star*, sixth and last volume of the autobiography.

1955   22 February, *The Bishop's Bonfire* opens in Dublin at the Gaiety Theatre, presented by and starring Cyril Cusack, directed by Tyrone Guthrie.
28 December, *Red Roses For Me* opens in New York at the Booth Theatre, presented by Gordon W. Pollock, directed by John O'Shaughnessy.

1956   February, undergoes a prostate operation at Torbay Hospital.

March, undergoes a kidney stone operation at Torbay Hospital.

March, publication of *The Green Crow*, a collection of essays.

October, publication of *Mirror in My House*, the two-volume edition of the autobiography.

27 December, *Purple Dust* opens in New York at the off-Broadway Cherry Lane Theatre, directed by Philip Burton, and runs for just over a year until 5 January 1958, the longest run ever for an O'Casey play.

29 December, his son Niall dies of leukaemia at age twenty-one.

1957   3 January, Niall O'Casey's ashes are dispersed in the Garden of Remembrance at the Golders Green Crematorium, London.

February, copies of the British edition of *The Green Crow* sent to Ireland are seized without explanation by the Irish Customs Office, resulting in an unofficial ban of the book for a year.

May, publication in Moscow of Russian translations of *The Shadow of a Gunman, Juno and the Paycock, I Knock at the Door, Pictures in the Hallway*.

September, publication of *The Bishop's Bonfire* in a Russian translation in *Zvezda* (Star), Leningrad, organ of the Union of Soviet Writers.

10 October, the Dublin Tostal Council accepts *The Drums of Father Ned* for production at the International Theatre Festival in 1958.

1958   January, the Archbishop of Dublin disapproves of a plan to present *The Drums of Father Ned* and a dramatization of Joyce's *Ulysses* at the Theatre Festival.

February, the Archbishop's attitude leads indirectly to the censorship of O'Casey, Joyce and Beckett, whose works are withdrawn from the Tostal Theatre Festival.

July, as an aftermath of the indirect banning of *The Drums of Father Ned* from the Dublin Tostal, he decides to ban all professional productions of his plays in Ireland, a ban he maintains until 1964.

12 November, *Cock-a-Doodle Dandy* opens in New York at the off-Broadway Carnegie Hall Playhouse, directed by Philip Burton.

20 November, *The Shadow of a Gunman* opens in New York at the Bijou Theatre, presented by the Actors' Studio, directed by Jack Garfein.

1959   January, he appears in a reunion scene with Barry Fitzgerald in the documentary film, 'Salute to the Abbey Theatre: Cradle of Genius', directed by Paul Rotha.

9 March, *Juno*, a musical based on *Juno and the Paycock*, book by Joseph Stein, music and lyrics by Marc Blitzstein, staged by Jose Ferrer, opens in New York at the Winter Garden Theatre.

25 April, *The Drums of Father Ned* opens in Lafayette, Indiana, the world première

presented by the Lafayette Little Theatre, directed by Jeanne Orr and Robert Hogan.

7 September, *Cock-a-Doodle Dandy* opens at the Edinburgh Festival for its first professional production in Britain, directed by George Devine, prior to its opening in London at the Royal Court Theatre on 17 September.

1960   1960   30 March, on his 80th birthday a group of 18 writers and theatre people in Dublin send him a silver tankard or 'tassie' of appreciation; and Samuel Beckett in Paris sends the following message: 'To my great compatriot Sean O'Casey, from France where he is honoured, I send my enduring gratitude and homage.'

1961   29 January, Sean O'Casey Pipe Night is celebrated at the Players Club in New York.

4 February, he refuses to accept an honorary degree of Doctor of Letters from Trinity College, Dublin.

June, publication of *Behind the Green Curtains, Figuro in the Night, The Moon Shines on Kylenamoe.*

26 July, *The Bishop's Bonfire* opens in London at the Mermaid Theatre, presented by Bernard Miles, directed by Frank Dunlop.

1962   16 August, *Purple Dust* opens in London at the Mermaid Theatre's O'Casey Festival, presented by Bernard Miles, directed by Peter Duguid.

5 September, *Red Roses For Me* opens in London at the Mermaid Theatre's O'Casey Festival, directed by Julius Gellner.

26 September, *The Plough and the Stars* opens in London at the Mermaid Theatre's O'Casey Festival, directed by Joss Ackland.

30 October, a double bill of *Figuro in the Night* and *The Moon Shines on Kylenamoe* opens in New York at the off-Broadway Theatre de Lys, presented by ANTA Matinee Theatre, directed by John O'Shaughnessy.

November, publication of *Feathers From the Green Crow: Sean O'Casey, 1905–1925*, a collection of O'Casey's early articles, pamphlets, stories, poems, and plays, edited by Robert Hogan.

4 November, *The Moon Shines on Kylenamoe* is performed on Irish television, directed by Shelah Richards.

1963   March, publication of *Under a Coloured Cap*, 'Articles Merry and Mournful with Comments and a Song'.

March, *Red Roses For Me* is performed in a German translation at the Deutsches Theater, East Berlin.

27 March, The Theatre Section of the Union of Soviet Writers in Moscow pays a special tribute to O'Casey on International Theatre Day.

July, The Lord Chamberlain bans a performance of *Figuro in the Night* at a Festival of Irish comedy in London.

1964   January, he lifts his seven-year ban on professional productions of his plays in Ire-

1964   land so that the Abbey Theatre can prepare for the presentation of his works in London at the World Theatre Festival in honour of the 400th anniversary of Shakespeare's birth.

20 April, the Abbey Theatre's production of *Juno and the Paycock* is presented in London at the World Theatre Festival.

27 April, the Abbey Theatre's production of *The Plough and the Stars* is presented in London at the World Theatre Festival.

August, suffers a heart attack and spends two weeks at the Torbay Clinic.

18 September, dies of a second heart attack at the Torbay Clinic.

22 September, his body is cremated in Torquay.

3 October, his ashes are dispersed in the Garden of Remembrance at the Golders Green Crematorium, London, in an area between the Shelley and Tennyson rose beds.

WORKS BY O'CASEY

PLAYS:

Collected Plays, Vol. I (1949), *The Shadow of a Gunman, Juno and the Paycock, The Plough and the Stars, The End of the Beginning, A Pound on Demand.*

Collected Plays, Vol. II (1949), *The Silver Tassie, Within the Gates, The Star Turns Red.*

Collected Plays, Vol. III (1951), *Purple Dust, Red Roses For Me, Hall of Healing.*

Collected Plays, Vol. IV (1951), *Oak Leaves and Lavender, Cock-a-Doodle Dandy, Bedtime Story, Time to Go.*

The Bishop's Bonfire (1955).

The Drums of Father Ned (1960).

Behind the Green Curtains, Figuro in the Night, The Moon Shines on Kylenamoe (1961).

Kathleen Listens In and *Nannie's Night Out*, in *Feathers From the Green Crow: Sean O'Casey, 1905–1925* (1962), ed. Robert Hogan.

AUTOBIOGRAPHIES:

I Knock at the Door (1939); *Pictures in the Hallway* (1942); *Drums Under the Windows* (1945); *Inishfallen, Fare Thee Well* (1949); *Rose and Crown* (1952); *Sunset and Evening Star* (1954). These six volumes are reprinted in *Mirror in My House*, 2 vols. (Macmillan, New York, 1956); and *Autobiographies*, 2 vols. (Macmillan, London, 1963).

SONGS, POEMS, PROSE AND LETTERS:

Songs of the Wren, 1st and 2nd series (1918); *More Wren Songs* (1918); *The Story of Thomas Ashe* (1918); *The Sacrifice of Thomas Ashe* (1918); *The Story of the Irish Citizen Army* (1919); *Windfalls* (1934); *The Flying Wasp* (1937); *The Green Crow* (1956); *Feathers From the Green Crow: Sean O'Casey, 1905–1925* (1962), ed. Robert Hogan; *Under a Coloured Cap* (1963); *Blasts and Benedictions: Articles and Stories by Sean O'Casey* (1967), ed. Ronald Ayling; *The Letters of Sean O'Casey*, 3 vols., ed. David Krause: Vol. I (1975); Vols. II and III are to be published in 1976 and 1977.

WORKS ABOUT O'CASEY

BIOGRAPHY AND CRITICISM:

William A. Armstrong, *Sean O'Casey* (1967), a pamphlet.
Saros Cowasjee, *Sean O'Casey, The Man Behind the Plays* (1963).

Gabriel Fallon, *Sean O'Casey, The Man I Knew* (1965).

Herbert Goldstone, *In Search of Community: The Achievement of Sean O'Casey* (1973).

Robert Hogan, *The Experiments of Sean O'Casey* (1960).

Jules Koslow, *The Green and the Red, Sean O'Casey – The Man and his Plays* (1950).

David Krause, *Sean O'Casey, The Man and His Work* (1960; enlarged ed., 1975).

Martin B. Margulies, *The Early Life of Sean O'Casey* (1970).

Eileen O'Casey, *Sean* (1971).

Peter Kavanagh, *The Story of the Abbey Theatre* (1950).

Andrew E. Malone, *The Irish Drama* (1929).

Sean O'Faolain, *The Irish* (1947; revised ed., 1969).

Robert O'Driscoll (ed.), *Theatre and Nationalism in 20th Century Ireland* (1971).

Arland Ussher, *The Face and Mind of Ireland* (1950).

BIBLIOGRAPHY AND COLLECTED CRITICISM:

Ronald Ayling (ed.), *Sean O'Casey: A Selection of Critical Essays* (1969).

Thomas Kilroy (ed.), *Sean O'Casey: A Collection of Critical Essays* (1975).

Sean McCann (ed.), *The World of Sean O'Casey* (1966).

E. H. Mikhail, *Sean O'Casey: A Bibliography of Criticism* (1972).

HISTORICAL AND THEATRICAL BACKGROUND:

Una Ellis-Fermor, *The Irish Dramatic Movement* (1954).

ACKNOWLEDGMENTS

Some of the biographical information in this volume is based upon material in my previous writings on O'Casey, as well as upon my personal contact with him during the last ten years of his life.

I am especially indebted to Mrs Eileen O'Casey for her dear friendship and good counsel, for giving me permission to use material from her husband's plays, autobiography, essays and letters, and for allowing me to use some of her family photographs. My debt to other individuals and institutions is acknowledged separately below.

Easter Week Rising, May 1916 – interior of the General Post Office, Dublin. Photo Radio Times Hulton Picture Library.

16 Two sketches by Sean O'Casey: *Dodging Bullets in Dublin during the Revolt* and *Scene in the Slums after the looting* from a letter to James Shiels, 17 July 1916. James Shiels, Dublin.

18/19 Sean O'Casey's tenement room at 422 North Circular Road, Dublin, where he lived from 1921 to 1925.

20 Sean O'Casey in 1924. Photo Radio Times Hulton Picture Library.

20 Sean O'Casey's letter to Gabriel Fallon, 1 October 1926, with a sketch of himself armed with pen and ink. Texas University Library, Austin.

21 Interior of the Old Abbey Theatre during a rehearsal. Photo G. A. Duncan, Dublin.

21 Sketch by O'Casey sent with a letter to Leo Rush, a carpenter in the St Laurence O'Toole Parish, October 1915. Leo Rush, Dublin.

22 The programme cover of the Abbey Theatre's production of *The Shadow of a Gunman*, 1924. *The National Library of Ireland, Dublin.*

23 Arthur Sinclair as Seamus Shields in a scene from the June 1927 production of *The Shadow of a Gunman* at the Court Theatre, London. Photo from *The Illustrated Sporting and Dramatic News*, 11 June 1927.

From the Raymond Mander and Joe Mitchenson Theatre Collection.

Eileen Carey as Minnie in a scene from the June 1927 production of *The Shadow of a Gunman* at the Court Theatre, London. Photo *The Illustrated Sporting and Dramatic News*, 11 June 1927. From the Raymond Mander and Joe Mitchenson Theatre Collection.

24 Arthur Sinclair as the 'Paycock'. Caricature by Hynes of *Juno and Paycock* at the Royalty Theatre, London, November 1925. From *The Illustrated Sporting and Dramatic News*, 12 December 1925. From the Raymond Mander and Joe Mitchenson Theatre Collection.

Cast list from the programme of the first production in London of *Juno and the Paycock* at the Royalty Theatre, 16 November 1925. From the Raymond Mander and Joe Mitchenson Theatre Collection.

25 Four scenes from the first production of *Juno and the Paycock* at the Royalty Theatre, 16 November 1925. Photo *The Illustrated Sporting and Dramatic News*, 28 November 1925. From the Raymond Mander and Joe Mitchenson Theatre Collection.

Sarah Allgood as Juno in the first production of *Juno and the Paycock* at the Royalty Theatre, London, 16 November 1925. From the Raymond Mander and Joe Mitchenson Theatre Collection.

27 Programme for the first production of *The Plough and the Stars* at the Abbey Theatre, February 1926. By courtesy of the Abbey Theatre, Dublin.

Sean O'Casey with Ria Mooney in the part of Rosie Redmond from *The Plough and the Stars*, 21 June 1926. Photo G. A. Duncan, Dublin.

28 William Butler Yeats. Caricature sketch from *The Abbey Row*, 1907. Courtesy of the Trustees of the British Museum.

29 John M. Synge. Oil painting by John Butler Yeats. Municipal Gallery of Modern Art, Dublin. Photo Barry Mason.

30 Sean O'Casey being directed by a policeman outside the Fortune Theatre, London, 1926. Private collection.

31 Sean O'Casey with Augustus John at the Chenil Gallery, Chelsea, 1926. Private collection.

32 Sean O'Casey and Eileen Carey on their wedding day, 23 September 1927, outside the Roman Catholic church of All Souls and the Redeemer, Chelsea, London. Private collection.

33 Lennox Robinson. Oil painting by D. O'Brien. *Courtesy of the National Gallery of Ireland.*

Lady Gregory with W. B. Yeats at Coole Park. Photo courtesy of Major Richard Gregory.

34 Lady Gregory, Sir Hugh Lane, J. M. Synge and W. B. Yeats. Pen and ink drawing by W.

Orpen, 1907. *National Portrait Gallery, London.*

35 Lady Gregory, co-founder of the Abbey Theatre. Cartoon from G. Plunkett's *To hold as t'were*, 1920. *British Library.*

36 Lady Gregory, 1852–1932. Oil painting by John Butler Yeats, 1903. *Courtesy of the National Gallery of Ireland.*

37 Coole House. Oil painting by Jack Butler Yeats. *Courtesy of the National Gallery of Ireland.*

The autograph tree in Coole Park on which Sean O'Casey carved his initials. Photo Irish Tourist Board.

39 The rejection of *The Silver Tassie* by W. B. Yeats at the Abbey Theatre. Cartoon by Charles E. Kelly from *The Dublin Opinion*, July 1928. *National Library of Ireland.*

Caricature sketch by O'Casey of the directors of the Abbey Theatre rejecting *The Silver Tassie*. Private collection.

41 W. B. Yeats. Caricature by Edmund Dulac, 1915. *Courtesy of the National Gallery of Ireland.*

43 Letter to C. B. Cochran from George Bernard Shaw, 23 November 1929, congratulating him on his production of *The Silver Tassie*. From the Raymond Mander and Joe Mitchenson Theatre Collection.

Flyleaf of *The Silver Tassie* inscribed to C. B. Cochran by Sean O'Casey, 1928. From the

Raymond Mander and Joe Mitchenson Theatre Collection.

45 Charlotte Shaw: photograph taken by George Bernard Shaw. By courtesy of Harold White.

46 James Joyce, 1852–1941. Drawing by Wyndham Lewis, 1921. *Courtesy of the National Gallery of Ireland.*

47 Abbey Theatre Programme and *The Abbey Row*: covers. Courtesy Mrs Lily M. Stephens.

48 Sean O'Casey in 1928. Sketch by Evan Walters. Private collection.

49 James Agate (1877–1947), drama critic, in 1943. Photo Radio Times Hulton Picture Library.

51 A scene from the New York stage version of *Within the Gates*, 22 October 1934, with Lillian Gish, Nat Johnston, Kathryn Colleen. Photo Culver Pictures.

52 George Jean Nathan. Photo Culver Pictures.

53 Eugene O'Neill in 1933. Photo Culver Pictures.

Brooks Atkinson. Photo Culver Pictures.

55 Sean O'Casey, aged 54. From an article, 'Sean O'Casey, Irish Patriot', by Joseph Alsop, Jr. in *Vanity Fair*, 1934.

57 Kingsley Martin. Cartoon by Low, *c.* 1930's. Reprinted by permission of the *New Statesman*.

58 Ethel Mannin. Photo Mansell Collection.

59 William Butler Yeats. From the Raymond Mander and Joe Mitchenson Theatre Collection.

61 Riversdale, Rathfarnham, near Dublin. Photo courtesy Shotaro Oshima, author of *Yeats and Japan*, Yeats Society of Japan.

64 Jim Larkin. Bust by Mina Carney. *Courtesy of the National Gallery of Ireland.*

67 Harold Macmillan. Photo Mansell Collection.

68 Title page of *The Flying Wasp*. Published by Macmillan & Co. Ltd, 1937.

69 Malcolm Muggeridge, April 1949. Photo Radio Times Hulton Picture Library.

71 Sketch by O'Casey for the spine of *I Knock at the Door*, drawn in 1939. Author's collection.

72 Sean O'Casey in his study with the photograph of Augustus John and himself above his head. Private collection.

73 Pope John XXIII. Photo Mansell Collection.

74 Caricature of Sean O'Casey, from an article, 'O'Casey Says', by Angus Drummond in the *Courier*, April 1964. From The Raymond Mander and Joe Mitchenson Theatre Collection.

75 George Bernard Shaw in Hong Kong, 1933. Photo P. A. Reuter.

78 Sean O'Casey at a rehearsal of

his play *Purple Dust* with the producer, Sam Wanamaker, May 1953. Photo Radio Times Hulton Picture Library.

79 George Orwell, October 1943. Photo BBC copyright.

82/83 The O'Casey family – Sean, Eileen, Niall, Shivaun, Breon. Photo W. Suschitzky, London.

84 A scene from the first performance of The English Stage Company's production of *Cock-a-Doodle Dandy* at the Royal Court Theatre, London, 17 September 1959. From the Raymond Mander and Joe Mitchenson Theatre Collection.

85 A scene from the first performance of The English Stage Company's production of *Cock-a-Doodle Dandy* at the Royal Court Theatre. From the Raymond Mander and Joe Mitchenson Theatre Collection.

88 Niall O'Casey. Photo Robert Emmett Ginna.

90/91 Sean O'Casey at his typewriter. Photo W. Suschitzky, London.

93 A scene from Samuel Becket's *Waiting for Godot* at the Arts Theatre, London, 1955. From the Raymond Mander and Joe Mitchenson Theatre Collection.

94 Sean O'Casey at his Torquay home. Photo Robert Emmett Ginna.

99 Sketch by O'Casey included in a letter to Timmie McElroy, the young daughter of William McElroy, best man at Sean O'Casey's wedding, dated 26 May 1928. Timmie McElroy, London.

100 Sean O'Casey in old age. Photo W. Suschitzky, London.

101 The O'Casey flat at 40 Trumlands Road, St Marychurch, Torquay. Private collection.

103 Sean O'Casey with Barry Fitzgerald. Photo W. Suschitzky.

105 Sean O'Casey in old age. Private collection.

INDEX